Also by Dr. Kidane Araya:

Business as Mission

ISBN 978-1-77354-352-9 Paperback

978-1-77354-352-9 eBook

Also available in Tigrina and Amheric

Put God First

Dr. Kidane Araya

Scripture quotations are not taken word-for-word from standard English translations.

Published by Kidane Araya, Edmonton, Canada

ISBN 978-1-77354-354-3 Paperback
978-1-77354-355-0 eBook

Also available in Tigrina and Amheric

Publication assistance by

PAGEMASTER
PUBLISHING
PageMaster.ca

Acknowledgements

BY THE GRACE of God, it has been a privilege to spend time during uncertain times of a global pandemic writing this book. I'm making the best use of this time reading, writing, and researching the topics already covered in this book. As the whole world is shut down and people are at home, we all have had time to spend time with family and reflect on what's important.

I have spent many years on the journey as a born again Christian and have learned quite a bit in that time. I wanted to share my experience so you can learn more about applying faith in our daily life. *Put God First* is a calling for all believers, and in this book, I expand on how and why we should live by this principle.

A special thanks to my beloved family. My wife Tsege Ghebretinsae and my children, Mizan Kidane, Bereket Kidane, Saron Kidane, and Abel Kidane. I would like to thank them all for the support and encouragement they have shown me. I would also like to thank God for all the blessings in my life. He is the author of my faith and I hope with this book we can reach out to many people. Thanks to all who have contributed to my faith and my life to shape this book.

God Bless.

Dr. Kidane Araya

Preface

PUT GOD FIRST is written with a focus on all Christians who follow biblical principles. I choose to write a book on this topic to lay a foundation on the principles of leading a successful and gratifying life. I have been thinking of writing a book on putting God first for more than a decade. I came to realize that if we do not put God first, whatever we do in life, including the meaning of our mere existence and purpose in life, are worthless. It is my prayer that through reading this book, you will understand the benefits of putting God first in your life.

I encourage all readers who desire to have a successful life to read this book with an open heart and mind and be willing to receive all that the Holy Spirit offers. The central message of biblical principles of putting God first, discussed in this book, is based on the teachings and character of Jesus Christ.

Contents

Trust in God 1

Identifying First is First 9

Daily Life with Christ 21

Obedience... 26

Live For Purpose... 33

You Are a New Creation... 39

Chapter 07: Do Not Compromise Your Faith 43

Focusing on Eternal Life 51

Understand the Purpose 58

Don't Compromise Integrity for Money or Fame 66

Evangelize Life.. 73

Be Generous to Others 77

Helping as Much as You Can 81

Stewardship, A Way of Life 88

About the Author 94

My son, do not forget my teachings, and keep
my commands in mind, because they will bring
you long life, good years, and peace.

Do not let mercy and truth leave you. Fasten them around your
neck. Write them on the tablet of your heart. Then you will find
favor and much success in the sight of God and humanity.

Trust the LORD with all your heart, and do not rely on
your own understanding. In all your ways acknowledge
him, and he will make your paths smooth.

Do not consider yourself wise. Fear the LORD,
and turn away from evil. [Then] your body will be
healed, and your bones will have nourishment.

Honor the LORD with your wealth and with the first
and best part of all your income. Then your barns will
be full, and your vats will overflow with fresh wine.

Do not reject the discipline of the LORD, my son, and do
not resent his warning, because the LORD warns the one he
loves, even as a father warns a son with whom he is pleased.

Blessed is the one who finds wisdom and the one
who obtains understanding. The profit [gained]
from [wisdom] is greater than the profit [gained]
from silver. Its yield is better than fine gold.

[Wisdom] is more precious than jewels, and all your
desires cannot equal it. Long life is in [wisdom's] right
hand. In [wisdom's] left hand are riches and honor.

[Wisdom's] ways are pleasant ways, and all its paths lead
to peace. [Wisdom] is a tree of life for those who take
firm hold of it. Those who cling to it are blessed.

By Wisdom the LORD laid the foundation of the earth. By
understanding he established the heavens. By his knowledge
the deep waters were divided, and the skies dropped dew.

My son, do not lose sight of these things. Use priceless
wisdom and foresight. Then they will mean life for you, and
they will grace your neck. Then you will go safely on your
way, and you will not hurt your foot. When you lie down, you
will not be afraid. As you lie there, your sleep will be sweet.

Proverbs 3:1-24 (God's Word Translation)

CHAPTER 01

Trust in God

"I HAVE A strong belief in God" is a statement you hear many people say. This is easily said, but it is quite challenging to believe in God when you are in hardship. In doing anything, we must establish our faith and trust in God. If we are not going to make this a habit, we are likely to get into trouble the next time we face a test or at the time of trial.

We may be free from anxiety and fear or make wrong decisions, which will hurt us and cause more pressure. Doubt will kill faith. This is why it is essential to living our lives in God's path and let him show us how to deal with any storm we may encounter.

To trust God is precisely where God wishes us to be. Proverbs 3:5 says, "Trust in the God with ALL your heart and lean not unto your own understanding."

So, the question arises of how and why we should trust God. I was raised in an orthodox background, but I accepted Jesus Christ as my personal savior 15 years ago. I want to share with you a lesson God has taught me and shown me in my Christian life. With all my heart, with all my strength to rest in him. Once I depended on him and put my trust in him, I began to understand his Word. As 1 Chronicle 29:12 says, "both riches and honor come from you, and you rule over all, and in your hands is power and might; it is in your hand to make great and to give strength to all." With this in mind, I continue to faithfully put my trust in him, because everything comes from him.

Surrender yourself to God

When you realize you can receive supernatural power from above, your outlook on life changes. You change from worry to worship by realizing that God controls every situation in your life. Let him be your master and everything in your life. Once you stop doing things with your own strength, God will take over and elevate you to new heights.

1. Replace destructive thoughts with positive ones

Your thoughts are very powerful and can affect your mood, attitude, and behavior. So, when you find yourself thinking negative thoughts that disappoint you; for example, not leaning on the Lord wholeheartedly, and relying on your own understanding, "In all your behaviors acknowledge him, and he shall direct your paths." (Proverbs 3:6).

Continue repeating that positive verse aloud until all the negativity is replaced with positive thoughts and superseded by the peace of God beyond all understanding.

2. Request God to provide you and bless you with patience

The truth is that God will help you at the right time. He will never disappoint you. During this time, you just need to keep praying because your faith will be tested one day. During the proceedings, ask God to give you tolerance and patience and help you believe he knows what works best for you. Remember, God is never late. He always appears on time.

3. Confidence in God

We must study the Bible regularly to have true faith in God and know that we can hear God. When we spend time reading and reflecting on the Bible, we develop a strong spirit. Then we listen to

God speaking to our hearts and begin making decisions based on what God leads us to do, not just what we think, feel, or want.

When you go beyond what you want, think and feel, and do it according to the words of the Bible and the will of God, you can develop good habits and destroy all of your bad habits. You come to a place where God's blessings — his justice, peace, and joy overflow your life.

4. *The absoluteness of God*

There is not even a single percent chance that God's word is not complete truth and absolute. The announcements he made are not sometimes true, or mostly true, but they are a hundred percent true. If even one small finding was not accurate, we would not be able to believe him. If even one percent were not true, we wouldn't know which part to accept as truth.

As a trusting Christian, I ultimately believe that God will settle everything, and this phrase helps me every time I pass through challenging times. Knowing I could completely trust his word gave me hope as I had never known. We trust in God as his word is true.

Pure from lying

Human beings lie. Unfortunately, even Christians lie. But God is infinitely holy. He only tells the truth. As we all know, Satan will try to make us question the authenticity of God. So, the question is, what do I believe in? Myself, my eyes, my feelings, or my evaluation of God's word? We can never fully trust anything from anyone except God, as he never lies. HE is pure from lying, and we can believe in the truth of God.

1. *God is the only one having all the powers*

We can make a commitment, then after promising, any situation can stop us from fulfilling that promise. I may agree to pick you up at 1:00 pm and then be unable on my way to your house and cannot show up. We can make promises and then other things happen that stop us from fulfilling our promises.

But nothing can stop God. He has sovereignty over every molecule in the universe. He has dominance over angels and demons, and everything present in the world. Satan and all his servants cannot stop God from saving people, providing us with food, and fulfilling his plan for us.

2. Cry to your God

Surrendering to God begins with our lips and thoughts. It needs more than relying on its commitment. We need to call him to show this dependency. "Recognize him in all your ways; he will make your way straight" Proverbs 3:6.

In prayer, we admit that his way is higher than ours. We show that we have left our troubles, burdens, and dreams in his proficient hands. In fact, he assures us when we pray to him, he will hear our voice, "In the evening, in the morning, and at noon, I cry in suffering, and I firmly believe that my voice is heard" Psalm 55:17.

We have given the keys of our lives to him, and we recognize he can lead us in the right direction. But for this thought to be implemented, we have to trust God.

3. Put God first in your life

Putting yourself first is the easiest; when something noble happens, we want to congratulate ourselves. When something terrible happens, we want to comfort ourselves by finding someone to blame. In other words, we often have a "self-centered" starting point. When it comes to money, the tussle is harder.

Solomon himself also has much wealth, but he knows that his money does not belong to him, "Worship the Lord with your wealth and plant all the high-quality crops; then your barn will be filled. And the barrel will be filled with new wine." Proverbs 3:9-10.

If we can fully trust God with our wealth, then we really show our dependence on Him. While this requires a great deal of faith and doing so means focusing on God.

4. Trust God's character

Even if you do not identify God's character, you must believe in it. This is another way to trust God. God does not demand or require us to fully understand or comprehend everything he does. If he wanted us to know all things, he could have revealed all the things for us to know. But instead, God gave us all the truth we need to know and relate to the world. We are humbly called to trust God based on this revelation.

Romans 9:20; Deuteronomy 29:29 Romans 11:33.

The Bible conveys clearly that God's character is perfect. So, when we think of the less clear reality of characters in the Bible, this must be our starting point.

God is ubiquitous

Sometimes we don't like to be alone. The person we love may have died, and we don't know how we would live without them, but God has promised that he will never leave us. *"Be strong and courageous. Do not be afraid or terrified because of them, for the LORD your God goes with you; he will never leave you nor forsake you."* (Deuteronomy 31:6)

When we find ourselves in trouble, we can take a deep breath and thank God that he is by our side. (Psalm 46:1) In this technology-rich world, I'm happy to learn that we don't have to text God and find him unavailable or call to find out if he is present. God is present 24/7. He encourages us to call him when we need Him. Putting our trust in God is going to him with whatever intentions we have on our minds.

Once we reach this stage of trusting God with everything, we will observe a significant change inside us. We begin to feel much more relaxed and patient. The anxiety and confusion will begin to disappear, and we will find real peace of heart just by trusting God.

1. Acknowledging God

Recognizing God means walking with God, no matter where we are or what we do. This means not only consenting intellectually but also in our behavior by perceiving his character and will at every moment of life.

If we are committed to trusting God and seeking God in all circumstances, does that mean life will be easy or not as difficult? We have all experienced enough to know this is not true. On the contrary, we can expect that our journey will eventually lead to difficulty, and when it comes, we will not be shaken.

Acknowledging God does not mean there will be fewer difficulties in life, but rather that these difficulties will be met fearlessly. We can easily face them by having faith in God. Even if we feel frustrated or that time is running out, it still is useful to his will.

When we have more trust in Jesus and have the confidence to act according to his wishes, we may have to turn down an opportunity that seems great because Jesus called us somewhere else or accepted the intimidating call. Recognizing God in everything means we remember nothing will happen to us beyond the will of the Father. Knowing this can give us strength even in times of difficulty, pain, and fear, because we know God will never leave us.

2. To trust is to fear the God

Be not wise in your own eyes; fear the Lord, and turn away from evil. (Proverbs 3:7)

Putting your trust in the wisdom of an ordinary man, looking to ourselves—both independently and corporately—is fruitless in the long run.

The wisdom of this creation is foolishness to God. For it is said, "He catches the wise in their own craftiness"; and a second time, "The Lord knows the thoughts of the wise, that they are futile." Hence, let no one brag about men.

No matter what we think we know, the Lord knows more. Not only does he have the ability to surpass our own wisdom, but he can also use it for larger goals. So, how can we learn to believe in God's wisdom and not ours?

The answer to "be wise in our own eyes" is to fear God and live in awe. The fear of God is uncomfortable for some people. They want God to be full of love and passion. But to truly understand the scope of God's love, you must realize that he is also watchful.

His holiness, size, ability, beauty, understanding, intelligence, and personality are difficult to understand. His anger at sin was shocking. It is so much so that the Bible records people falling as if dying just by God's appearance.

The cure for us being held back by our own knowledge is in identifying how sublime and yet fearsome our God is. The fear of God not only makes his loving-kindness that much more amazing but also motivates us to avoid immoral activities in all their forms. For what desirability can sin hold in the face of such a fearsome Lord?

3. To trust, is to accept life from Christ

"It will be soothing to your flesh and refreshment to your bones. (Proverbs 3:8)"

Trust in the Lord and be in awe of his healing. The term for flesh here is only used in two other verses in the Bible. In one place, it means "umbilical cord," and in the other place, it means "navel." As a result, the healing spoken of here has a connotation of birth, as if trust in the Lord is equivalent to a **rebirth**.

The author of Proverbs then compared the images of birth and death. Trusting and fearing the Lord is like drinking water to dry bones. It echoes chapter 37 of Ezekiel, where God's word restored the Dry Bone Valley. He combined birth and death with their words and used them as a prophetic metaphor for how the Holy Spirit poured out to his people.

It doesn't matter what pain or suffering you are enduring. Jesus knows. He can use them for our benefit and glory in ways we cannot understand. Even if the hope seems to disappear, it can unexpectedly provide treatment because our hope is on it.

The perfect trust of Christ

Trusting in the Lord is the only way to fully live. Nothing is more completely reflected in life than the work of Christ. Throughout his life, he trusted the heavenly Father completely, even to death. Through his work on the cross, his resurrection, and ascension, he provides us with new life and injects his Holy Spirit into our hearts.

In a culture of erroneous trust, promise-keeping, and loss of life, only Jesus is unchangeable and invincible and worthy of us all. Only he trusted the Heavenly Father wholeheartedly, paving the way for our salvation, so we must also trust him. As long as we acknowledge him in every way, God will provide healing, wisdom, and love to the world through Christ.

CHAPTER 02

Identifying First is First

WE LIVE IN a fast-paced world. Usually, we are distracted by the way God designed our lives. Ephesians 1:11-12 says, "In whom also we are assigned an inheritance, having been foreordained according to the purpose of him who works all things after the counsel of his will." In Christian life, put God first and everything else will follow. The word of God in Matthew 6:33 says "but seek first the kingdom of God and his righteousness, and all these things shall be added unto to you." But people leave what is first and prioritize what follows. In my opinion, this is a lack of knowledge of the word of God.

As a firm believer in Jesus for many years, and a full-time and part-time evangelist in the world abroad for the past many years, I have been seen to grow faithful. Here are some questions to ask yourself: Do I want to live for him today? And, "How does he want me to help others live for him today?"

The Bible is a fairly long and complex book that contains many stories, characters, thoughts, challenges, details, and so forth. But at the same time, we definitely see consistent themes and patterns. The purpose of this book is to define some of the fundamental priorities God has for his people, from the beginning to the present day. So, every morning when we wake up, we should readjust our mindset to suit God's expectations and purpose for each of us.

We can start on any day. It can be a day of work, relaxation, or remodeling at home, or in one of our favorite places. This can be a day spent with our family, friends, colleagues, neighbors, or strangers. We aim to increase our understanding and ability to recognize daily how to best manage our lives, for the fruit of the kingdom and the glory of God.

Here are a few priorities set aside by God, which I believe are the foundation of the Bible and can underpin our daily lives. Are there any magic numbers? No! As we grow in Christianity, are there other important ideas and priorities? Yes!

The basic priorities in life

1. Spiritual dependence:

Every day, every moment of our time, we keep our "mind under the control of the Holy Spirit" and our "synchronization with the Holy Spirit," allowing the Holy Spirit to guide us throughout our day and in everything we do. God has always wanted his people to establish intimate relationships, communication, and humble dependence upon him.

We have seen it from the beginning of humankind with Adam and Eve at the very beginning of creation. We have seen how God related and conversed with Israel over the centuries. And, we have the most intimate and powerful expression as Jesus died on the cross to make it possible for us to be pardoned and cleansed of our sins so we could become a holy place with the Holy Spirit and the Lord living in us.

2. Remorse and purity:

Living a holy and clean life before God is essential for us to release the fruit of the Holy Spirit, to please the sanctuary and to bring glory, and to maintain right relationship with God.

From the beginning, we saw God longed for and asked his

people to live a holy and pure life. In the Old Testament, God made it possible to restore right relationship through the sacrificial system. And then, sacrificed his son's last sacrifice as the one-off answer to our struggle against sin. Now we can live with humility and repentance every day. When we sin and fail to put Jesus in the middle, seeking becomes difficult for us, and if we quickly turn to Jesus for forgiveness and restoration, we can get it effortlessly.

3. Learning and stewarding:

Managing our time, money, talent, relationships, work — in all the ways, we are blessed and suitable as a nourished son of God and Jesus' disciple. Learn daily to bring all life under the authority of Jesus and the truth outlined in the Bible.

God had a close father-son relationship with Adam and Eve because he used to spend time with them every day to help them learn to behave the way he did. We see God continued to play this role concerning Israel, as God had sent prophets and other great leaders to teach, remind, encourage, and challenge people to learn and continue to grow following God's purposes and priorities. Then Jesus gave us a final example. He called on his disciples to follow him, as learner/students to act in his way, and learn to rule all life for God's sake and God's will.

4. Loving as family:

We must Love our missionary/evangelical community and most churches in the family. They often preach the gospel to one another through serving, generosity, sacrifice, encouragement, listening, prayer, truth, and reconciliation.

God has always wanted his people to live such a loving, serving, generous, compassionate, and welcoming life together. The whole world will notice this and be strongly influenced by their example and quality of life. He hoped this would be true of Israel, and we see this hope continuing in Jesus, the disciples, and the early

Church. Through much of Paul's teaching, it is clear we should be a continuous expression of loving as a family.

5. *Loving as missionary servants:*

By loving daily and preaching the gospel to family members, neighbors, colleagues, classmates, and people who we meet through hobbies and our children's activities, we align with intentions of GOSPEL.

God not only intends to make his people a loving family but also a loving family to all who connect with him. He has always wanted his people to become priest families, help families, share the gospel, show the gospel to everyone, and preach the gospel to them, no matter where they go, at every opportunity.

***

These five priorities are vital to our daily lives as obedient and fruitful disciples, and these disciplines help us follow the path of Jesus and give us a allow us to become more like Jesus. Consider making these priorities something you are always praying for yourself and others, regularly encouraging yourself and others, and holding each other accountable.

Setting right priorities is vital to our success as Christians, but even some very passionate Christians are surprised by the true teaching of the Bible in this respect.

As children born of the Spirit of God, we prepare to enter the Kingdom of God. We are about to graduate and be introduced to the family of God to help rule the world under Jesus Christ. But we have to qualify for the captain position. To help us succeed, we need to prioritize time.

The Apostle Paul recognized how essential it is to identify the value of our time, "And do this, knowing the time, that now it is high time to awake out of sleep; for now, our salvation is nearer than when we first believed" (Romans 13:11). The less time available, the valuable it becomes. And, as time is running out for every person reading, we must be very cautious about prioritizing the time and using it wisely.

Prioritizing averts "wreckage"

How do Christians suffer from spiritual wrecks? If you do not have your priorities in order, you will quickly head for wreckage. Some people look away from their targets and lose sight of where they are heading. They confuse their priorities and soon find themselves stuck. When it comes to walking in Christ, you can't look away from the spiritual light and not crash.

To succeed, we must put our priorities in the right order and pay close attention to each item. Otherwise, when fiery judgment comes, our spiritual home can be burned. We may be left with only the foundation, and this hardly guarantees our salvation.

There are some essential priorities in a Christian's life. The first is God and our personal relationship with Him. If we give any of the other preferences first place, it's like putting the cart in front of the horse, so this is where we start.

1. Loving and pleasing God

In the vertical direction of life, the overriding priority must be love and pleasing the Lord. Jesus is most concerned with his relationship to his heavenly Father and honors him throughout his ministry on earth. Jesus said of the Father, "I always do what pleases him" (John 8:29), which shows the personal priorities in his life. To please the Father is the ultimate wish of the Savior, and he must be in your heart. Paul wrote in the letter, "We encourage in the Lord Jesus ... how do you walk and please God. First of all, pleasing God must be your priority. How to achieve this?

If you wish to please God, you should know him first. When Jesus prayed, he confessed the ultimate goal of humanity is to know the Heavenly Father. Jesus prayed, "This is the unending life, that they may know you, the only true God, and Jesus Christ who sent you" (John 17:3). God wants you to know him personally and experience his presence and eternal life.

Once you know him personally, you must obey his commands, which will lead you to God's plan of life. This is why Jesus ordered his disciples to adjust their priorities, so he could add all the blessings he had intended to their life. He commanded, "First of all, seek the kingdom of God and his righteousness, all these things shall be added unto you" (Matthew 6:33). If Jesus declares that God and his kingdom must be the first, then there is no doubt in your mind what priority you should consider. The only question is, does God and Kingdom now occupy first place in your life?

Most Christians intellectually agree that Christ must be first, but there is no reflection in their daily behavior, decisions, and choices. Jesus said to his disciples, "But why do you call me 'Lord, Lord', but don't do what I say?" (Luke 6:46). If you do not follow Jesus' instructions, he clearly not the first in your life.

If you see that Jesus and his kingdom are not true priorities, turn to him immediately and seek his forgiveness, and choose this job to serve him. His life and love will begin to fill your soul. Do it now!

2. The spouse

Of all relationships and accountability on the horizontal, your spouse must be first. It is essential to establish this from the beginning because you have to deal with multiple relationships throughout your life. Children, parents, friends, the ministry, and your work are stressful. How do you determine that your spouse should be the first?

The husband was commanded to follow Christ's example and asked to commit himself to love his wife, just as Christ valued the church and gave himself up for her (Eph. 5:25). And, of course, women should love and obey their husbands with equal self-sacrifice and love. If Jesus orders you to put your bride first, then you should also put your spouse in your heart and give your relationship priority above all others. These tips should solve the problem of who should appear first.

However, if you allow your child, mom or dad, government department, work, or hobby to take this priority, you will not please God, and you will have a conflict with your spouse. Why? Because when your partner looks at your priorities, he or she will see that someone or something is more important to you than the one.

The Bible is clear on this point. There is only one person on earth called flesh, and that's your spouse. From the beginning, God declared, "Therefore, a person will leave his parents and be with his wife and become one" (Genesis 2:24). This passage shows that the relationship between husband and wife is more important than all other relationships.

A marriage relationship goes beyond your relationship with your parents or children. Yes, you are from your parents, but one day you choose to leave and marry your spouse. Yes, your children are from your physical body, but they are only temporarily at home. One day, they will leave you and marry someone. This fact proves the couple's enduring relationship must take precedence over the parent or child.

3. The children

The child must take the next rank in your order of priority because of the needs of immediate family members. The Bible teaches we must, "First learn to show godliness at home ... for this is good and acceptable before God" (1 Timothy 5:4). Our first ministry is to discipline our children before we try to serve anywhere else. Why? Because our children are the essential disciples in the kingdom of God. The poet announced that God had ordered all fathers to train their children according to God's word so that "future generations can recognize them, the children who are about to be born so that they can appear and declare it to children so they can settle. Hopefully, do not forget God's actions, but keep God's commandments" (Psalm 78:5-7). Solomon also called his wife to discipline, for Solomon used his mother as the family guide. "My son, listen to your father's instructions, and don't forsake your mother's teaching: (Proverbs 1:8). If you serve everyone and accumulate possessions but don't try your best to win your child for Christ, what is the benefit?

4. The services you offer to the church

Some of you may wonder why I didn't call this part "Worshiping God"? Let me explain. If you love the Lord and seek his kingdom first, love your spouse as the church of the love of Christ, and train your children to become his disciples, then you will serve the Lord in a very real and effective way.

However, many pastors, elders, deacons, Sunday school directors, Sunday school teachers do their best to serve the church, but fail to fulfill the first three priorities I discussed in the chapter. You may be a church servant and rarely spend time on personal prayers and Bible study. You may be a church servant and, at the same time, have a terrible relationship with your spouse or child behind the door. However, Jesus always makes people and relationships more important than activities. Jesus stopped everything he was doing and talked to a woman at the well or to someone who touched him Mark 5:25-34). Here's an example of priorities!

If you are reading this book now, and you serve church in a certain capacity and place this service above your spouse or children, listen to what I say. This will not continue forever. When your services to church have a higher priority than the people in your family, you have to pay something. Your marriage might suffer, and your children might be angry with you. Even your ministry will become difficult because when your home is not functioning properly, it is difficult to serve others. You will be the one who is unhappy. Your relationship at home must come before church. This is why Paul insisted that one's house must be neat and orderly before allowing a person to be a church leader. Paul said this person should be, "A person who can manage his own house well and his children obey with respect (because if a person does not know how to manage his own home, how will he take care of the church of God)?" (1 Tim 3:4-5)

After your house is in order, you can find a place where you can use your gifts to glorify God. If your own home is not arranged, you should adjust your priorities.

5. The job or business.

Your service to God is more important than your work or business because you are a citizen of the Kingdom of God first. Paul proclaimed, "Because our citizenship is in heaven, we also anxiously await the Savior Jesus Christ from there" (Philippians 3:20). However, you will spend more time working or doing business because you need to make a living.

However, many people say, "I don't have time to serve the Lord, go to church, or do housework because I have to support my family." I agree it is imperative to support the family, but if there is no time to serve God or your spouse or child, something is wrong. Why am I so sure? Because no one will spend every minute at work or in the workplace. A person will always have time to do other things that are important to him or her.

If you do not take time with God or your partner, then you have to put these other things first. This mistake will only make your entire marriage and spiritual life unhappy and hopeless. Jesus highlighted this when describing what would happen to a person with the wrong priority. Note what Jesus says makes a person's life unproductive, "The care of this world, the deception of wealth, and the desire for other things make the term endless, but the result is fruitless" (Mark 4:19).

Do you allow other things to stifle your relationship with the Lord or the life that marriage brings? If you wish to have a fulfilling life and a happy marriage, then you need to change your priorities.

6. Accountability in the home

There are many conflicts in marriage because one or both partners cannot fulfill their responsibilities at home. When a spouse is
unwilling to help in child upbringing and discipline or is unwilling
to help with housework or unable to provide help when needed, the
marriage will naturally produce resentment and eventually lead to
conflict. Why? Because all marital partners know they are part of
a team, everyone must become the servant of the other. These were
the oaths when sworn. We all promise to love, respect, protect, and
serve our partners. Being a servant follows the example of Jesus. He
said, "Whoever wants to be a great man among you, let him be your
servant" (Matthew 20:26). Jesus also said that he did not come to
live but to serve (Matthew 20:28).

Do you want to be a servant at home? If so, then when you
are asked for help, give love to your spouse (Psalm 5:13). When you
do this, your home will be filled with companionship and love, and
this love will only increase.

7. Friends

Relationships with friends other than your direct family must
always be on your priority list. You need good friends. In fact, the
Bible teaches that we need a "friend who is closer than a brother"
(Prov. 18:24). It is difficult to find such good friends.

However, the Bible also teaches that your spouse must be the
best friend in life. Solomon's wife said to her husband, "This is my
dearest love, this is my friend" (Song 5:16). Of course, in the vertical direction, when you feel unfriendly, the Lord is your ultimate
friend. Jesus said, "You are my friend" (John 15:15). However, many
people tell me they have better friendships with people at work or
church than with their spouses. Sometimes this is because your
spouse has rejected all your attempts to develop friendship. You can
only pray that their hearts will change. However, if you realize that
you have not made your partner your top priority in friendship and
have spent more energy and time with others than your partner,

then turn around and adjust your priorities. Work hard together, take time to chat, and find romantic time with your spouse.

Many times, couples become lazy when making friends. If it is you, reverse the direction immediately.

8. Leisure pursuits

Prioritizing is very important in your Christian life. You have to prioritize all areas of your life, including leisure activities. Leisure is important, but you can't let it take precedence over God, church, and family. For example, if your leisure activity is participation in team sports, or a community meeting takes precedence over your wife and family, this will cause conflict at home.

I've seen members of political teams who meet two or three nights a week, but don't understand why their spouse gets frustrated when they don't want to be with their family on the weekend. If you don't prioritize family life, your marriage and family relationships will erode.

How to transform into a good person

Make a list of your priorities

When a couple came to consultation, they found they struggled with their priorities. The first thing they should do is to make a written list of all the activities. This list helps them understand exactly what they are doing.

I recommend the couple to prioritize this list together. This allows them to see if their priorities are consistent with their own values, faith, and the word of God.

Make a decision

If a couple or individual is over-committed to different activities or over-committing time to some efforts, they need to decide how to modify, or remove some activities from the list. There are many things that we give our time to that are good things, but they are not essential and can be very damaging to the overall health of marriage and family. These are difficult but essential decisions to make.

When a couple adjusts their priorities, their personal lives and marriage begin to experience the blessings God intends to bring to their home. I have found that people can restore harmony in marriage and relationships by adjusting the time allocated to work or spending time with friends or entertainment.

I found others that needed to take a more radical approach because they were too involved in other things, so survival of the marriage was threatened. They must completely remove a few items from the list. That is, you may have to stop playing on the second softball team or stop going to the family party to buy kitchenware, so you can spend time with your spouse or children.

Keeping the right order

We have seen that there are four priorities at the top of the list, for the sake of: 1) God, 2) family, 3) work, and 4) church.

If we balance these priorities without ignoring any priorities or putting them in the wrong order, we can expect to stand before the Holy Spirit, shining in glory, and bring glory all of humanity to earth. Peace, happiness, and prosperity!

CHAPTER 03

Daily Life with Christ

WHEN IT COMES to faith, we find ourselves longing for spontaneous, accidental interference from God, sudden enthusiasm to tell Jesus to strangers, or overwhelming peace in a crisis. While these are marvelous proofs that God plays a role in our lives, there is still much to be said for trivial ordinariness every day.

If we are to establish a strong and significant faith and relationship with Christ, then a routine is essential. When we think about how we define our daily work in many other areas of life, it makes sense to extend it to our spiritual life.

We are in-part defined by the jobs we have. Likewise, being Christian, we must set some activities in our lifestyle to reflect our faith. If we are full-time Christians, then our daily activities should reflect this identity. If we are Christians, then our Christianity should be visible.

Here are some essential ways we can practice every day to help make this our reality.

Immerse yourself

Immerse yourself — instead of succumbing to the fictional God of nothing or the irony of comics, and those who hate God, or to inject self-blame criticism — indulge in the Bible, conscience, creativity, and it's the ultimate self-expressing Christ in the Bible. Experience that wonderful, brilliant, almighty, magnificent, innermost, perfect God; who spoke the blessings of the Sermon on the Mount, and who died for the sins of the world — drive out the pagan idols of our culture's captivation with making gods of our own imagination..

Allow him to leave you in wonder.

Spend time talking to God

Most of us talk to someone every day, but not everyone can say the same about the frequency of talking to God. Leave some space in your diary to meet God during the day, even if you thank him for the glorious weather for a few minutes. If the weather is good, you can be in a quiet place in the park, where you can let its creative beauty — birds fly freely, trees flutter in the wind — stimulate your prayers.

Pray

Prayer is our personal relationship with God. We can talk to God just like we would talk to a father. Also, you can recite the prayers that Jesus gave us through his disciples. "Our Heavenly Father, may your name be holy. Your kingdom will come, and your will be done on the ground like heaven. Give us daily bread today. When we forgive those who sin for us, please forgive our sins, do not bring us to temptation, but save us from all scourges." Rehearse it and use it as a means of prayer.

Read the Bible

The Word of God provides obstacles for us to build faith, so we must remain familiar with faith. If you can't read or reflect on a large number amount at once, don't stop, shorter passages can have a big impact. From this beginning, we need to move on to larger portions. Why not opt to set some time aside for the word of God instead of wasting time on Facebook or Instagram.

Spend 5 to 10 minutes every day to understand the life and love of Jesus in our daily lives. Meditate on God's Word. Our God lives in us. Only through Jesus Christ can we discover Jesus in us, not through desires and thoughts, but through his perfect principles. Everyone is precious to Jesus. God has always wanted us to live happily. Develop good habits of reading Christian books, watching spiritual programs, and helping one another.

Follow Christ's teachings

The pearls of wisdom of Christ are brought to us in the Bible and by churches. God asks us to rest and meditate on the Sabbath. Join Sabbath services to give thanks to our God for saving us from hardships and troubles.

Honor our God

Praise, give thanks and give to our companions, who are also dedicated to God. He is almighty, massive, immense, and is always present everywhere, including his spirit in you. We should thank him for his life every day. Love is God. He invites us to live the life of his kingdom. It is on us to accept or reject. Accept his open arms.

Bless somebody with an unexpected act of kindness

As Christians, we strive to express our faith at every opportunity. Good deeds are one of the many ways we put faith into practice. Try to be more attentive to the needs of others. If it's a friend who has had difficulties at school, you can provide a side job, or you can help by taking part of lunchtime to explain their course outline; or you can help someone struggling with the family.

Love your neighbors

When we love our neighbors, we love ourselves. Even if everyone lives in a different body, we are together in Christ. The gift of God's love brings happiness, success, patience, harmony, peace, integrity, honesty, friendship, and hope.

Write a thank-you note

Just as we ignore the humble things that people do for us every day, it is easy to do this in God's blessing. Send thank-you emails to people who have always been by your side. In a brief space of time, you can express your appreciation for them, which will have an enormous impact on their lives. This can be symbolic or straightforward. If we take it as part of our daily routine, we will soon see how many blessings God has given us. When we pray at the end of the day, we also have many thoughts of thankfulness.

Stick to goodness and righteousness

Doing good by doing good (in Christ's way) is in itself a big deal. Without justice, you will fail. We will overcome all injustice by strength in Jesus. Our Lord has conquered the world forever.

What you say may differ from other people's ideas. What you say may differ from what you hear. Therefore, we should consider and cooperate to understand each other's views and live passionately.

Forgiveness

Always forgive others, fear God, and fight the good fight of the faith.

Never hate the people who betrayed, hurt, abandoned, or abused you. Holding a grudge is not good for you. It will only make you bear the burden of anger, frustration, or sadness, and drain energy over and over again (at times for years) in the inner life of the mind. The way to forgive is to reflect on your forgiveness. Once you realize you deserve hell instead of Christ, any action against you can be forgiven. This forgiveness will then direct you to service, not retreat when you are hurt again. If you live in awe of God, then you will find that the wisdom from above does not please the eye but pleases God. Only such views can give you strength to fight for good faith.

Follow the unfashionable virtues

In every age, some biblical virtues are more acceptable than others. Today, you are unlikely to be banned for preaching love and tolerance. However, if you talk about perseverance and humility, your approval rating may decline. Now, this does not mean you should push these qualities to other necks without having to do the work of translating their meaning into our folk today. This means you have to follow these qualities yourself and then discover their true meaning from the inside.

Use your mind

Someone once said we are a culture of thinking with emotion and listening with eyes. When someone wants to know about your situation, they don't ask, "Tell me what you think about it." They say, "Tell me how you really feel."

Our culture believes that the true self is the sum of our feelings rather than our thoughts. Logic, rational inferences, elaborate arguments, and deductive chains are considered less true than the emotional tear that keeps you awake. The important thing is that while our feelings do matter, they are not our nature. Furthermore, if you are upset about something, it does not necessarily mean that the matter is against you.

Today, Christians are criticized for believing in things that are neither rational nor scientifically verifiable. But, more ironically, as our culture becomes deeply embedded in the profound doctrine of emotion, these criticisms are rising more and more. Living a God-centered life is your calling and control as a Christian. So first, seek his kingdom and follow his glory. When you do this, you will find a fulfilling life.

CHAPTER 04

Obedience

OBEDIENCE BRINGS ETERNAL blessing forever. We believe Christ's obedience is our follow-ship with God.

Everybody loves family—it's a valuable relationship which the Lord has allowed them to shape. God has provided everyone with a "family"—a community in which people love—like a small-scale version of heaven full of contentment and happiness.

From a spiritual perspective, we are all members of a spiritual family. We have a divine father, a spiritual mother, and spiritual brothers and sisters. The Bible teaches that the command "love the Lord your God with all your heart, soul, and mind", is the first and greatest commandment, and the command to "respect your parents", is the first commandment with promise (Matthew 22:37 -38; Ephesians 6:2). According to Bible teaching, we should respect and serve our spiritual and physical parents.

What do parents want from most of their children? When children obey their wishes, they will feel delighted. Likewise, our heavenly Father wants us to follow him. Let us reflect on our beliefs and explore the relationship between faith and obedience through-out the Bible.

Faith becomes perfect through obedience

Faith is a vital part of our spiritual life. Without faith, it is impossible to please God, and any spiritual change could not occur. So, faith is an imperative factor in our life.

The Bible defines perfect belief as "faith in the company of action," not just a verbal expression of faith (James 2:14-26). Here, action means obedience to God's Word. Faith can always be measured by service. Obedience is the visible manifestation of invisible faith. The fundamental factor that destroys the relationship between God and humanity is disobedience. God ordered Adam and Eve not to eat from the tree of good and evil, but they disobeyed the Lord and touched the forbidden tree. Consequently, their relationship with God was broken, and they were expelled from the Garden of Eden (Genesis 2-3).

The sin of Adam and Eve recorded in Genesis is a shadow and is an excellent example of how we committed sin and have fallen to earth. So, what should we do to restore our relationship with God? Our disobedience has separated us from God. Therefore, we can only approach God when we obey God.

When Jesus came into the world to save humanity, he also set an example of obedience. Although a son, he learned obedience from the suffering he suffered. Once perfect, he became the source of eternal salvation for all who obeyed him, and God designated him as the high priest of Melchizedek.

Jesus was born to be God. Jesus came into the world by making himself the Son of God and living a faithful life that obeyed God completely (Isa. 9:6; Phil. 2:5). He educated us that obedience is the most important factor in the relationship between heavenly parents and children.

The Bible says that Jesus cultured obedience from his suffering and became perfect. Without obedience, our faith cannot be perfect. Romans had also stressed that obedience leads to human salvation.

Jesus' pattern of submission

The night before Jesus was executed, he went to Mount of Olives to celebrate the Passover and prayed eagerly there. Here we can see Jesus remembering obedience deep in our hearts.

"'Father, if you want, take this cup from me; but not my will, but your accomplishment.' A heavenly angel appeared in front of him and strengthened him. In pain, he prayed more desperately, his sweat like blood dripping on the ground" (Luke 22:42-46).

Jesus knew he would suffer on the cross, which caused him great pain. The Bible says that his sweat is like blood dripping on the ground. How serious and sad he must pray! Even in such great pain, he prayed, "Not my last wish, but yours." He accepted the pain, shame, and even death, to obey.

Jesus gave us all these examples that we should follow (John 13:15). By setting an example of washing our feet, celebrating the model of Easter, the example of keeping the Sabbath, and the example of keeping all the Father's will, Christ personally showed us the path of faith we should take.

Those who obey can enter heaven

With the influx of vast amounts of information every day, many people today tend to view and judge things from a common-sense perspective. So, even though God said it, they are reluctant to do what they don't like. Even among those who admit to believing in God, many adhere to their own ways and place them above the Word of God.

It is impossible for us to follow God if we live only for ourselves. If Christ only lives in us, obedience is stress free. As we have an everlasting hope, we can joyfully follow God's word. To fully obey God's commandments, faith must be present. It is impossible to keep them without obedience. Jesus also said that only those who do God's will can go to heaven.

"Not everyone who says to me, 'Lord, Lord' will enter the

kingdom of heaven, but only the one who does the will of my Father who is in heaven" (Matt 7:21).

Obedience is God's will. Only those who obey God's orders are going to enter into heaven. No matter how long distorted doctrines not found in the Bible are observed, we must change once truth is clear. Are the responsibilities of those who obey God's word right?

The redeemed are the people who follow the Lamb wherever he leads them (Rev 14:1-5). God has said he is prepared to punish every act of disobedience when obedience is complete (2 Co 10:6). Considering the allegory where Jesus said he would divide people from one another as a shepherd splits the sheep from the goats, we can see obedience through faith is something the sheep has. As God said, "My sheep attend to my voice".

The most imperative criterion for differentiating between the righteous and terror on the day of God's final judgment is whether or not one obeys God's word (Matt 25:31-46; John 10:27). That's the reason Christ came to this earth. And Christ lived a life of comprehensive submission to Father, even to the point of death.

Our predecessors proved their faith with obedience

Faith and obedience are inseparable, and true religion can always be proved by obedience. If a person is confident in his faith but does not obey the words of God, then he cannot be said to have faith.

Those who have faith always obey the words of God. One day, God called Abraham to test his faith by ordering him to sacrifice his only son, Isaac. It was difficult for him to sacrifice his precious son. He was born at the age of 100. However, Abraham immediately obeyed the command of God. He did not ask, "How can you take my son, who I begged for 100-years? Please allow me to offer another sacrifice?" Instead, he took Isaac and immediately went to Mount Moriah. Isaac went up the mountain and asked, "Father,

there is fire and firewood, but where is the lamb for the burnt of-
fering?"

Can you imagine how Abraham was feeling at the time? He
answered, "My son, God will provide the lamb for the sacrifice."
When they reached Mount Moriah, Abraham was ready to sacrifice Isaac, as God had asked him. At that moment, he heard the
voice of God saying, "Abraham! Don't put your hands on the boy.
Now I know how big your faith is because you didn't turn away
your son, your only son. Abraham experienced the most difficult
test of his life by obeying God, and he was greatly blessed by God
(Gen. 22:1-18).

Noah also had great faith. At the time God commanded him
to do something beyond human understanding, he built the ark as
God told him to. His actions upheld his faith and saved himself and
his entire family (Genesis 6-7; Hebrews 11:7).

At the time of Joshua, the Israelites marched around Jericho
seven times and yelled on the seventh day, just as God had ordered
them to do. What happened? Some people may be thinking, "If we
walk around the city and shout out loud, will the city walls really
collapse?" But when they obeyed God's commandments, something
amazing happened.

We live in a three-dimensional domain, so we cannot fully
understand how God works in the world. This is why we must obey
everything God says. We may not know God's will immediately,
but we certainly will realize it in time (Joshua 6; John 13:7).

When they left Egypt, the Israelites were in a dilemma. The
Red Sea was in front of their eyes, and the Egyptian army pursu-
ing them from behind. God ordered Moses, "Raise your staff and
stretch your hand across the sea to divide the water." When Moses
raised his staff, the sea was broken so that the Israelites could cross
the sea safely (Exodus 14).

Our ancestors proved their faith by obeying God. When they
obeyed God's word, the amazing happened — Joshua's invasion of

Canaan, Gideon's victory, Moses' miracles, and so forth. There is no obedience where there is no faith and where there is no conviction without the work of God. This is God's will, shown to us throughout the Bible.

Obedience brings all blessings

How did Abraham and Noah show their faith? How did the faithful apostle Paul demonstrate his faith? All of them proved their faith by obedience. Christ obeyed God and even died. He was perfectly made, above all creations, and his name was above all. This is a noble title, above angels and all the other spiritual people in heaven.

If you obey the Lord your God completely and obey all the commandments I give you today, the Lord, our God, will set you high above the nations of the earth. If you obey the Lord, your God, all these blessings will come to you and go with you. You will be blessed in the city and blessed in the land. The fruit of the womb is blessed, and the harvest of the land and the young animals are blessed. Herd calves and flock lambs are blessed. Your kneeling basket and trough will be blessed. You will be ultimately blessed when you come in and be sanctified when you go out. Although, if you do not obey the Lord your God and do not obey all the commandments and decrees that I give you today, then all these curses will come to you and exceed you. Deut 28:1–19.

The fruits of obedience are blessings, and the consequences of disobedience are curses. The costs of obedience and disobedience are definitely different, just as the Bible says, "A man reaps what he plants."

The Israelites encountered many difficult situations on their journey through the desert. Do you think God led them through the wilderness without food and water because he was incapacitated? Of course not! The Bible says, "For the past 40 years, God has led you to walk in the wilderness, to humble and test you to understand whether you are deep in your heart and willing to obey his commandments" (Heb. 8:1-2).

During our journey of faith through the spiritual wilderness, we may also encounter various difficult situations. Whenever this happens, it is important to remember the journey of the Israelites through the desert. Just as God proved Abraham's faith, he also tests our faith to know whether we obeyed him.

Godly fathers and mothers came to save their children, the people of Zion. Let us obey them and follow them wherever they lead us, believing firmly that their teachings will lead us to eternal life and heaven. When the eternal kingdom of God is approaching, we must have faith and obedience.

God measured Abraham's faith, Noah's faith, Gideon's faith, and Joshua's faith through their service. We should continue to improve our belief quotient through obedience to God. Considering what happened in the past, let us fully observe the good teaching of God and receive every blessing from God.

Siblings in Zion! I sincerely ask you all to have more faith, like Abraham and Noah. The first fruit that pleases parents in heaven is worth boasting in the presence of angels and all other spiritual life in heaven and uniting together so that you receive the Kingdom.

CHAPTER 05

Live For Purpose

LIFE IS A journey. Inevitably, we are all going to the end of our life. We either walk through life without a sense of direction, or live with goals and achievements. The game has started. Where have you planned on going, and what have you planned to do?

Everyone's life is driven by something — internal anxiety, angst or fear, insecurity, anger, resentment, their past, possessions, parents, money, and so forth. God wants us to be intentional and goal-driven. The world is driven by his plan. The meaning of life is realized when we have goals. Before the Lord even planned the world, he planned you. In the process of planning you, he laid out goals for you, even before you were born. When you achieve goals in life, you will bring glory to God and bring satisfaction to yourself.

Jesus was a man with a goal. He said in John 17:4, "I have completed the work that you have done for me, and I will bring you glory on earth." If you are a believer, you want to bring glory to God. How did you do that? You do this by completing the work God has done for you. [Other related verses: Ephesians 1:5-11; 3:11 Rome 8:28 2 Titus 1:1 Pro 29:18]

Different levels of living

You live life at one of these three elementary levels:

1. Survival. The first layer or type (the bottom layer) is the survival layer. Many people live in survival mode. They are living life most casually. They are not enjoying real-life; they just exist. They spend their time, make some money, and spend the weekend. They never have real-life goals or motivation.

2. Success. Most individuals are in the second level of living, a little higher stage called the success level. The focus of this level is on paying off the mortgage or instituting a comfortable lifestyle. Yet, this level does not provide satisfaction.

3. Significance. Significance is the level when you realize why you're here on earth. You have a determination for your life. You know that your life has a substance. You distinguish that there is a purpose behind what's going on in life. People living in significance recognize what on earth they're here for!

How to find a Purpose-Driven Life

Identify what's important to you

Purpose flows from values. Whenever we decide on life, whether or not we realize it, we filter the decision through a "value grid". Values affect everything we do. We all have values, but we often fail to explain or verify them.

Where do you get values from? We choose music from parents, peers, magazines, books, the music we hear, and society as a whole. Today, one of our methods of acquiring values is through the media, particularly television.

The Bible tells us that the values of the world are well known and have not changed. We will gain the value of life from the world or the Bible. You will gain a lifetime's worth of culture or Christ. "Do not love the secular longing for physical pleasure, the longing for everything that attracts you, and the pride of wealth and importance — these are not of God, but of the world" (1 John 2:16).

Pleasure or happiness is one of the top three values in this world. If you ask most people, "Have you ever thought about life?" They say, "I want to have fun." I want to be pleased—I want to feel good. These are different ways to express happiness. Today, the entertainment industry is one of the largest industries. We are a culture of pleasure.

Possessions include the drive to buy everything that appeals to you. Our society is consumed by consumerism — clothing, cars, houses, jewelry. We hope everyone can see what we have. We collect things and buy things that are not needed, but we will continue to buy them. Our self-worth is based on our net worth.

Prestige or power, rank, and popularity. In our world, image is everything. We place great importance on identity. We want individuals to look up to us. We want people to think that we are important and successful and that we are valuable.

Romans 12:2 says, "Do not follow the pattern of this world anymore, but change for the sake of mental renewal. Then you will be able to experience and approve God's will — his kindness, pleasure, and perfect will." The Knowledge Bible says, "Do not adapt too well to your own culture, or even integrate into it without thinking."

If you align with the world system of values, then the ultimate value of life is pleasure, possession, and prestige; and you not be able to experience the will of God for your life. Think about your values and where they will take you. Think ahead! Don't wait for a crisis or great pain to come before you consider your life. Ask yourself, "What lasts?" Think, 10 or 20 years from now to forever.

1. Happiness will not last. Hebrews 11:25 says, "The pleasure of sin will only last a short time."

2. Possessions won't last. 1 Tim.6:7 says, "We carried nothing into this world, and we can take nothing out of it." When the millionaire dies, how many assets does he leave? He leaves everything!

3. Prestige will not last. Mark 10:31 states, "Many who appear to be important now will become the least important in eternity."

Solomon had everything, but departed from the will of God's life (see evangelization). His collection? "I tried my best." But this is pointless and useless. It is all emptiness. If you have no goals in your life, then these things do not matter. The bottom line is, "The world and its desires (the value of the world) will disappear, but those who do the will of Lord will live forever" (1 John 3:17).

Define real purposes for yourself

There are three fundamental aspects to God's purpose for your life:

To be God's friend

God says he created us to know that he loves us. The Bible says, "God is love" and he made you purely to love you. God wants us to be his "friend". Luke 7:34. John 15:13-15. James 2:23.

Matthew 22 says, "Love the Lord your God with all your heart, with all your mind. This is the first and greatest commandment." He said this was a priority. He said that if you do nothing in your life, you need to know and love God.

Father God is calling for you. He hopes to institute a close relationship with you. You will be asked to join his family. You are his son or daughter. He wants to love, care, provide, and protect you. God wants to be with you. This should be our highest purpose or requirement and will become the basis of any other "ministry".

To help others

First, you must be a friend of God. He wants to establish a personal relationship with you. Then, God wants you to begin to "obey" his will by helping others. What is my life contribution? That is, the talents he provided me to use?

Ephesians 2:10 says, "We are God's workmanship, created in Christ Jesus, and we can do good deeds (without watching too much television), which God prepared for us in advance." Our motivation is not to gain redemption or to promote ourselves, but to benefit others because of God's love in our hearts. You are contributing to the earth, not just taking up space. You are put on this earth to heal and make some contribution to life. God planned you before you were born. You have a purpose!

1 Peter 4:10 says, "God has given each of you some special abilities. We must use them to help one another and pass on God's blessings to others." We're here to help each other.

The Christian life will become one of the "servants". It is the key to true greatness. The servant considers himself "weak" and seeks to make others successful (Mark 9:33-37). Christ was a servant. He served us as a servant and gave his life. He told the disciples that they should also serve just the way he served. "Do what I have done to you" (John 13:15). His mission is a servant's mission, as is ours (Mark 10:42-45).

To influence your world

Mark 16:15 says, he ordered them, "Go into all the world and address the good news to all creation."

Go to all God's creatures and announce the good news about Jesus Christ. The world includes all facets and places where individuals live and interact.

Jesus lives in the "world". He walks around in various sections of socio-religious leaders, tax collectors, children, people in need, sinners, people of all backgrounds, and different classes of society. He was the "friend of sinners" (Matthew 11:19). He was with them. They saw his life, heard his words, and felt his heart. He was with them, but it didn't affect his lifestyle or character. See Luke 5:27-32.

How to achieve the purpose

"Inconsistent values" is a primary source of stress — believe one thing, live another.

Three aspects show our true values:

The **schedule** – Where do you spend your time? Devotion time every day, church party? Each week we have the same amount of time — 168 hours. Everyone reading this book has the same time — 168 hours a week. During this week, those who made their lives vital, and those who coast make management choices. We all have the same time, and its use shows our values.

The **budget** — where do you spend your cash? Taxes, giving?

The **relationships** — who do you run with? Family, church, unchurched?

Eliminate all the worthless things that don't matter at all. Avoid doing what you feel is not important, so you will have time to find the real purpose.

Life's purpose is perhaps one of humanity's deepest aspirations. Many celebrities have reached the end of their career and declared success meaningless. There seems to be no deep demand for success. Philosophers and psychologists try to solve the imminent goal problem — to a large degree, there is no fully satisfactory solution. We have spent countless dollars trying to achieve our life goals.

I have tried here to condense everything and tell the importance of finding a purpose in Christ.

CHAPTER 06

You Are a New Creation

WITH HIS DEATH on the cross, Jesus Christ consummated a perfect revitalization for us. God honored his Son and promoted him to the very throne of this universe. God has declared Jesus Christ as *"Lord of all"*. Jesus Christ is the only one having authority over this universe and earth.

Jesus Christ is the superintendent of God's new family.

God not only made Jesus Christ the master of all the people but also made him the leader of a new family — the "children of God". We were born into Adam's sinful family. Adam is our head. We shared everything about him and what Adam had done. When we were reborn spiritually, God did a pleasing thing for us. He took us out of Adam's sinful family and brought us into the family of Christ. Christ is now our head. We share everything about him and everything he does.

Christ is the foundation of God's New Creation

Not only does God have a new family in the world, but he also has a new creation. Christ is the beginning and end of God's new creation. God's old creation was destroyed by sin. Satan is known as the "prince of this world" because he is the invisible ruler of a world system based on desire, greed, and power.

The Bible says that Jesus Christ "gave himself for our immoralities, that he may deliver us from the present sinful world, as per the will of God and our Father." (Gal 1:4)

To save us, Christ came to the place of our sinful world. He himself was innocent, but on the contrary, he replaced us. Our sins fell on him. He died and was buried, but on the third day, he stood up again in a glorious new resurrection.

Other things happened too. He was brought up in a brand-new spiritual world — God's new creation. Christ is no longer in this world. He is the beginning and head of God's new creation. When it comes to Jesus, the Bible says that he is "the beginning, the eldest son raised from the dead; that he may have a superior position (first place) in everything. (Colossians 1:18) God now has his second person before him — a new person in a new place!

God's absolute salvation

For us to recognize God's absolute salvation, we must consider our situation before we were saved. When God saw us in our lost condition, what did he see?

He saw three things:

He Saw our sins. The evils that we have done.

He Saw our sinful self. The evil is who we are. We sin.

He Saw me in a sinful world. The Bible says in *"this present evil world"*.

Now, let us understand how God has dealt with each of these three things.

God dealt with my sins through the valuable blood of Christ

The only solution for our sins is the blood of Jesus Christ. Because Jesus shed his valuable blood for our immoralities and sins, we are forgiven for all our sins. The Bible states,

"The blood of Christ Jesus his Son purifies us from all sin." (1 John 1:7)

God deals with our sinful life by putting us in Christ

Just like there was only one remedy for our sins, we only have one treatment for our sinful existence. That treatment is death! The Lord's word states, *"The souls that sin shall die."*

How does God deal with my sinful self? He treated my sinful self by putting me in Christ on the cross. The Bible says, "Of him (Lord) are you in Jesus Christ." (1 Corinthians 1:30). God placed us in Christ on the cross. Our "old man" (our sinful self) was crucified with Christ. When he died, we died with him.

The Bible says, *"Knowing this, that the old self was executed with Him..."* (Romans 6:6)

How can we be crucified with Christ? Consider this illustration to help us understand. Let's cut a dwarf out of a piece of paper. Now, put this little guy in a book. The little guy is in the book now.

Suppose we put the book on the table. Where's the little guy? It's also on the table because it's in the book. Assume we put the book on the floor. Where's the little guy now? He's on the floor. Suppose we strike some keys on the piano with the book. Where's the little guy now? He plays the piano.

Now suppose we pack the book and send it to another country. What about the little guy? He went to another country because he was in the book. Again, we put this book underwater. What about the little guy? He also went underwater. Anything that happens to the book will also happen to the little guy because he is in the book.

When God protected us all, he put it in Jesus Christ on the cross. What happened to him also occurred to us because we were in Jesus Christ.

God carried us into his new creation

Now take a look at the most wonderful truths in the whole Bible. When Christ converted from the old creation to the new creation, he took us. Why is this happening? This is true because we are in Christ.

After Christ's death, we died with him. When Jesus was buried, we were buried with him. When he rose, we rose with him. Through our death with Christ, we get rid of the old creation. When Christ was resurrected in God's new creation, we were resurrected with him in God's new creation.

The Bible says, "*Thus, if anyone is in Jesus, he is a new creature; the old things are dead; behold, all things have become new*" 2 Corinthians 5:17.

A more accurate translation of the first part of this verse is: "*Therefore, if anyone [be] in Christ, [there is] a new creation.*"

Christ is God's. newly created, and we are in Christ. Therefore, if someone is in Christ, then he is a new man in God's new creation. As Christians, the most important thing for us is to understand is that we are new people in God's new creation.

The Bible says, "*God made us grow together and made us sit together in the sky of Jesus Christ.*" Ephesians 2:6.

What place do we have in God's new creation? We are with Jesus Christ because we are in Christ. We were in Christ when he died; we were in him when he was resurrected from the dead, and we were in him when he was elevated to the right hand of God as God's new head.

The Bible says, "*But, because we love him deeply, he loves us deeply, loves him, even if we die in sin, he also makes us live with Christ- through grace, and you are saved! We are with him in the heavens of Christ Jesus.*" (Ephesians 2:4-6 Net Bible)

CHAPTER 07

Do Not Compromise
Your Faith

DESPITE HARD SITUATIONS, we should praise God in advance for all his blessings. For some people, it's easier said than done. For other people with faith, this is easy to do. To have the life we feel we deserve, we often believe we can compromise our beliefs, belief systems, and moral values. We believe it is okay to turn away from God and refute his promises to prove we are doing it ourselves and bringing our own success and happiness.

However, no matter what the answers are, we may never understand the question of reasoning. We must never compromise on behalf of human or secular property or any belief that would cause us to oppose our beliefs. Nor should we let anything stop us from believing that God is our source of supply and in control.

We may be depressed, disheartened, or sad. But we should never be afraid of what the enemy thinks he can do. It has nothing to do with me or you. Even if we can't see it, it is about the glory of God. Only he has the power to control things.

After receiving some annoying news, I found myself worrying

about why people are doing such jobs. I thought, as a Christian, we are free from all the sufferings of the world.

I'm sure many of us may not want to feel unwell, but this may be best for us because God may be working through us. Perhaps God is preparing something more for us.

When I asked myself, "What happened?" My reaction to the news left me confused, shocked, and quiet. Facing opposition, truth and credibility replace fear. With every problem, I firmly believe that this is just a test of my faith.

Later that night, I was angry. Something came over me. I was afraid and felt depressed. I could not see the truth of God. I questioned God as Job did, because he didn't appear what I wanted or expected. I learned that I can only put effort into something, and the rest is in the hands of God.

Knowing that this was not my usual behavior, I asked God for help because I felt the enemy was assaulting me and trying his best to destroy me.

I told the enemy, "You know I am committed to God. You cannot steal my joy! Fighting is all around me. You are full of anger to destroy me. I do not want to engage in spiritual fights anymore. But this battle is not mine, but the Lord's. He will win."

After talking to my friend who prayed for me, I tried to fall asleep when night fell. I fought with the idea that even as a Christian, I am not immune from enemy attacks. I remembered had I read a few days earlier, "Faith in Christ brings great blessings, but also often brings great pain. God calls us to promise rather than comfort. He promises to pass on the suffering, to be with us, not let us get out of pain." This allowed me to rest.

The following day, I remembered, "We live in a corrupt world where people firmly believe they are the masters of their destiny. However, God announced another plan, that is, despite the hatred of the enemy, he desires to prosper us, not to harm us. No matter what others do, there are always some people who try to keep us away from him."

Attacking an individual's credibility spreads lies and falsehoods. Who are we to attack the credibility of God's truth? We can't do like bad people. "For we do not fight against flesh and blood, but the principality, power, dark rulers of the world, and spiritual wickedness in heaven" (Ephesians 6:12). This battle is not our battle. But the Lord's. Fight for all the armor of God!

God does not make mistakes. He is not a person who should lie or a man who should change his mind. Will he talk and then not act? Will he promise rather than deliver (Numbers 23:19)? His reputation is perfect. His words are reliable. God is righteous, he will do things well. He will punish wicked people and reward believers in darkness and light.

"Faith in God will not make our troubles disappear; it makes them look less awful because it puts them in the right angle." Acts 5:15-17

Things may not happen as we expect. Count all the joy. This is a blessing. The session is not over; it has just begun. God has laid the foundation for future development.

People may lie and pressure you. Remember, they did the same to Jesus, who died on the cross for you. But he did not lose faith. Christ did not compromise his faith in God. We are also subject to the same behavior and laws. Following his example, you will go further. Don't be content with things you don't believe. Do not sacrifice your faith for the benefit of others. You are not owned by anyone. You should do what you believe. Keep faith. God will reward you.

"People who are willing to follow righteousness, those who obey the law and seek it wholeheartedly, are happy. They do not compromise with wickedness, you have asked us to observe your orders." Psalm 119:1-4.

To compromise faith is to allow or make room for someone

who disapproves of a prevalent set of standards or rules. It is clearly mentioned in the Bible that God does not excuse compromising his morals or standards, "Happy are individuals of integrity who follow the instructions of God. Pleased are those who follow his laws and search for him with all their hearts. These are the people who do not compromise their faith with evil, and they walk only on God's paths. You have charged us to keep the commandments cautiously" (Psalm 119:1-4).

The terms *happy* or *blessed* define individuals of righteousness; those who are wholly submissive to the Lord's will and passionately devoted their whole life in a relationship to God. We must not compromise or stray from his morals but "march only in his path."

We heard God's voice (1 Kings 18:21, John 8:47, John 10:27), and we did not return to or permit any deviance from his word (Deuteronomy 4:2; Psalm 119:128, Revelation 22:18-19). Not compromising faith requires our unshakable submission to God, irrespective of the world's allowance to godlessness (Joshua 24:15, Psalm 119:10, Psalm 119:15).

As Christians, we must, "See to it that no one takes you imprisoned through dead and misleading philosophy, that depends on human tradition and the general principles of this world instead of on Christ" (Colossians 2:8; see also Hebrews 3:12). Individuals are also ordered to be "equipped to make a defense to anybody who asks you for a reason for the confidence that is in you. (1 Peter 3:15).

In simple words, we are ordered not only to remain truthful to the Word of God but to protect it, guard it and correct those who are in disapproval of it (2 Timothy 2:24-25). Lord is serious about our not compromising on Faith with the artificial standards of the world—the reason being that those outside of Christ might then "come to their right minds and escape the trap of the devil..." (2 Timothy 2:26).

Also, there are those individuals who confess to being Christians yet live their lives not in keeping with the teachings of

God, i.e., compromising their biblical principles by living like the rest of the world. As per them, the materialistic things of the world and its physical temptations take preference over the Word of the Lord (Acts 20:30; 1 John 2:16-19). Christ referred to these individuals as "those who heard the word, but the carefulness of the world and the faithlessness of riches and the desires for other materialistic things enter in and choke the word, and it evidences fruitlessness" (Mark 4:18-19).

Though admitting to following Christian values, such individuals compromise their faith by craving the artificial success of this world and tributes from their fellow man. Jesus penalized such people who modernized their dubious behavior, "How can you have faith when you receive glory from one another and do not seek the magnificence that comes from the only God?" (John 5:41-44). In simple words, to compromise on faith in one's total loyalty and commitment to God is to allow the temptations of this world, with all of its problems, to take preference over Christ (Matthew 6:24).

In what ways do we compromise our faith or the Word of God?

» *Upon failing to accept the Word*: "For the time is coming when individuals will not tolerate sound teaching, but have itching ears they will gather for themselves teachers to suit their own desires and will turn away from the teachings of God or listening to the truth and stroll off into myths" (2 Timothy 4:3-4).

» *Upon placing our desires before the Word of God*: "Although it remained unsold, did it not remain your own? And after it was sold, was it not at your removal? Why is it that you have forced this deed in your heart? You have not lied to mankind but to God" (Acts 5:4).

As faithful Christians of Christ, we must admit God's Word as a total inerrant reality (2 Timothy 3:16). We should be fully submissive to his Word (John 14:15; 1 John 5:3; 2 John 1:6). We must identify that his Word is not to be compromised for any purpose or anybody (Deuteronomy 17:11; Proverbs 24:7; Revelation 3:15).

A person's greatest strength is usually also the source of his greatest weakness. Someone with strong faith, if he does not pay attention, will boldly defend the truth of God, which will become cruel or rude. On the other hand, a person full of love and compassion will tolerate everything and everyone and make mistakes, thereby damaging the truth of God. In my opinion, the latter error is a more common danger in the church. Typically, Christians compromise with the world in the name of love and out of the desire to promote unity.

Have you heard the story of a man who was not sure of which side he wants to fight during the Civil War? He wore a coat from the north and pants from the south. Guess what? He got shot from both sides! This is what happens to people trying to live in two worlds. This is a painful place. Unfortunately, there are many in the church today that live a compromised life.

The Bible gives us an example of such a church in Revelation 2, Pergamum, the capital of Asia Minor. Pergamum is famous for its idiosyncratic idolatry. The houses of the altar of Zeus are the center of Caesar's worship. Worship of idols, evil, and sexual immorality were common. Pergamum's sin is his tolerance of evil and a "one size fits all" philosophy.

Unfortunately, this is what most people want today. Of course, they want to go to heaven, but they still want to live in sin. They want to party and commit crimes, commit unethical behavior, lie when necessary, cheat, steal if it suits them, hate and take revenge when they are crossed.

This is the idea of sin, telling yourself that God will understand. If you think you can achieve your inner satisfaction without repentance, and you think you are an exception to the rules, and you can repeatedly violate God's commands, then you are deceiving yourself.

I am not saying that Christians cannot sin. The Bible clearly states, "If we say that we have no sin, we will deceive ourselves, and the truth is not in us" (1 John 1:8). There are those who sin with regret and do not want to continue to do so. Also, there are some people who persistently, deliberately, repeatedly sin and then say, "It's alright. God will forgive me."

The Bible says, "Shall we sin to increase grace? Never! We die for sin; how can we live in it again?" (Romans 6:1, NIV) The devil introduced a compromise to the church of Pergamus, which he will present to people's lives today.

If you look at the sin in your life, you may go back to a series of mistakes — the small compromises you made led to the big compromise that caused you to collapse. As compromise enters the church, it weakens us.

I am not suggesting that we are hypocritical of you. Instead, we should live in such a way that unbelievers can look at us and say, "That person has some differences. Some are pleasant and admired." Sometimes they laugh at you. But they may respect you deeply in their hearts. On the other hand, those who have compromised have lost respect.

Compromise begins with separating from your first adoration for Jesus Christ. This compromise ultimately leads to dishonesty, adulation, idolatry, and other sins. Show me an individual who is not living in close companionship with God, and I will show you a person who is on the way to greater difficulties. It is just a matter of time.

The best antidote to the temptations and enticements of this world is a passionate love connection with Jesus Christ.

If your relationship with God breaks down, it is only a matter of time before you lower standards everywhere. Stay alert. Get close to Jesus and let the flame of first love burn brightly, and you will be strong. You will see that you have the power and determination to live a life that pleases God.

Sources of compromise of our faith

What stimulates us to do wrong even when we know what the right thing is?

Fear of being criticized. As we live in a society where people claim they have the right to do whatever they want, it is undoubtedly essential to represent our Christian faith or tell them what God thinks of their actions. *Fear of being rejected.* If we direct our beliefs and lives by Godly beliefs, people who follow their wishes may not accept us. However, sacrificing the standards of justice to please others will only result in the loss of everything God has planned for us. It is far better to live for Christ and follow his commandments so that we can get the best from God.

Fear of losing friends. Sometimes we are reluctant to hold on to our beliefs because we may lose our friends. But any friend who makes us depart from the Lord is not a genuine friend. As God's people, no matter the consequences, we should strengthen our convictions and beliefs. Our first task is to please Christ so that we can stand in the judgment of loyalty to him and his word.

What conditions or circumstances might motivate you to destroy your beliefs? Having a long-term perspective on the truth of Christ and his words will help you courageously strengthen your faith. So, make sure you take the Bible firmly and be prepared to defend your beliefs against the enemy — because a firm and determined Christian is the kind of person he wants to be.

CHAPTER 08:

Focusing on Eternal Life

"WHAT WILL IMMORTALITY or eternal life look like?" At first glance, this is an unusual question because it seems to be asking for something unresolved. However, eternal life is not only a future state, but it starts from this world and then continues beyond.

To better understand this concept, we must first ask, "What is Eternal life, and how is it obtained?" Everyone will experience eternal life. Heaven or hell, it is just a question of where you are going to spend it. This chapter will focus on eternal heaven.

Jesus is one of the keynote speakers on eternal life. In the final prayer before his arrest and trial, Jesus prayed for his disciples, "Now this is eternal life: that they may know you, the only true God, and Jesus Christ whom you sent" (John 17:3).

In his first letter, the apostle John wrote, "This is a witness: God has given us eternal life, and this life is his son" (1 John 5:11).

Eternal life in heaven is attained through the knowledge of the Father and knowledge included in his son Jesus Christ. We were given the gift of life through salvation, and God gave it to all through the death and resurrection of his son. When Jesus was beaten, humiliated, and crucified, the punishment for our sins was fully paid, and we have the opportunity to reconcile with God. Only by believing can we have this privilege. When we believe what his son Jesus died on the cross, God will accept his perfect record on our behalf.

New life starts right at the moment when we believe. We were immediately transformed into new creations; a new existence began, and we now live with God. This is the source of eternal Christian life. Now, God is always with us to direct us, guide us, and help us live according to the standards and principles contained in the Bible. But what will eternal life look like?

Although this kind of life is from now on and blessed by God, we still live on earth and suffer from earthly suffering, sadness, and disappointment. We take refuge in God, and the promises in the Bible comfort and sustain us. However, the life we gain is eternal. It goes beyond the boundaries of earthly existence, even beyond time and the grave. So while we may now suffer from adversity here as foreigners in foreign countries, we hope to have a better day.

Yes, Christians suffer in foreign countries because our new life exists contrary to those around us. They continue to live in darkness, without the life of Christ. The apostle Paul fully understood this because he wrote in a letter to the Corinthian believers, "If in this life only we have hope in Jesus, we are of all man the most deplorable" (1 Corinthians 15:19).

However, our hope is not only in this life. We look forward to an era where we will not be bound to earthly bodies and disadvantages of this life. The ultimate realization of eternal life will appear before the joy of the eternal God. We will transform into immortal life; we no longer need to worry about illness, suffering, or death. Expectations are even more remarkable than this. This is an inconceivable concept for the earthly mind, but the truth is provided to us by God's Word. "Dear friends, now we are children of God, our lives have not yet been known. But we know that when he appears, we will be like him because we will see him" (1 John 3:2).

The eternal life of a believer is a glorious and endless experience shared with Jesus Christ, for we are the "joint-heirs" of Christ. We will rule as kings and priests for life, and it is worth seeing the face of God in the end. Moreover, as the apostle John concluded, "everyone who hopes will purify himself as if he was pure" (1 John 3:3).

Once more I am here to focus your heart, and your mind, on the words of Christ in John 3:16, "For Lord so loved the creation that he gave his only begotten Son, that who believes on him should not just pass away, but have eternal life." Such words advise us about the threat we are in without Christ—perishing. Such words hold out the great hope of God's design to save us from perishing—it is his love that sent us his Son. In this book, we have focused on the duties that link us with the love of God—believing in his Son. We also direct our attention on destiny before us if we believe—eternal life.

Not affected at death

Death does not disturb eternal life. Jesus said in John 11:25, "I am the resurrection and the life; even if I die, those who believe in me will still live." Not all who claim to believe in Christ will find eternal life. Think of it as meaning, "everyone who receives eternal life by faith will transcend physical death."

Born again is full resurrection

When our bodies are resurrected from the dead and reunited with our souls, our transfer to eternal life will be completed. Jesus said in John 6:40, "This is the will of my father. Anyone who sees his son and believes in him can live forever; I will be resurrected on the last day." As he said (11:25–26), It's not just life, but resurrection as well. *Everlasting and forever.*

Eternal life will last forever. Does thinking about that make you tremble? So much of your eternal life depends on your spiritual awakening in this life. I heard a preacher once describe it in the church, If a bird flies from the ocean coast to a great plain and deposits a particle of sand once every thousand years and will keep on depositing that particle for the rest of life, that is everlasting.

An intimate relationship with Lord

This eternal life is a special relationship with God, the Father, and Jesus Christ the Son. Jesus defined eternal life as such in John 17:3. He prayed to his father in heaven and said, "This is eternal life. They know you, the only true God, and the Jesus Christ you sent." Eternal life is an intimate knowledge of God. It's not like being vaccinated against the disease of death, it is a conscious experience of knowing and connecting with God.

Eternal life: a destiny

In John 10:10 Jesus says, "I came that they may have life, and that they may have it amply". Have it in ampleness and have it endlessly. So, we believe that eternal life is Jesus's aim at Christmas. That is the gift given to humanity. I want you to have your eternal life and to know what it is and to enjoy it and to understand it.

The life is in Christ

John 1:4, "There is life in it, and that life is the light of man." And, in John 14:6, Jesus says, "I am the way, the truth, and the light." First and foremost, Christ is the Son of God. He is also known as the Word of God. Therefore, it is supernatural. This is not something humans are born with. We take it as a gift (cf. 17:2; 10:28), and supernatural behavior is beyond what we can do. We don't have any control over it. The life of Christ is eternal. "There is life in it, that life is the light of man."

Eternal Life is the word of God

Such life comes to us through the Word of Jesus.

Peter said to Jesus in John 6:68, "To whom do we go? You have the words of eternal life" (cf. 5:24). Christ's life is conveyed to the world through his words. He called himself the Word of

God. "The Word was the Word from the beginning, the Word was with God, the Word was God ... The Word became flesh and dwelt among us" (John 1:1, 14).

When he was on the earth with us, he spoke the words of life. He taught his pupils how to teach it. He said others would believe it through their words (17:20). Thus, eternal life extends from Christ to others through Christ's Word. It draws people to Christ Jesus. In hearing the words of eternal life, God draws individuals to Christ.

As per the verses in John 6:44, Jesus said, "Nobody can come to me unless the Father who sent me appeals to him." Jesus is where eternal life is received. We come to him if we want to have it (5:40). The word of God tells us how to have this life and introduces us to it.

But John 3:20 labels how, by nature, we hate the light of life. We don't want to come as we are laid naked and uncovered by the light of life. Our only hope is the sympathetic "drawing" of God. He overcomes our hatred for the light and opens our eyes to start seeing Jesus for who he actually is.

You might have seen the bumper sticker, "Start looking motorcycles." That's not because individuals aren't seeing them in one way. The reason is, they need to see them in another way. So, it is with Jesus at a very altered level of seriousness. Individuals know about him, but they don't actually see him for who he is, or they would be stunned with his greatness, beauty, control, goodness, understanding, and love.

With the help of eternal life in our lives, we can actually start seeing Jesus, and that is what Lord's drawing us does. It allows us to open our eyes to start seeing Jesus we already see in the Word.

Believing in Christ

We achieve this by believing in God

When we listen to the words of life and respond to the drawing power of the Lord, and believe in Christ; we receive him in our lives, and with him, we get eternal life because he is the eternal life (John 14:6).

As per the verses in John 15:5, Jesus said, "I am the vine you are the brushwood." In simple words, by trusting in Christ, we are unified to him the way a branch is combined with a vine—so that the life of the vine flows into the branch. The eternal life flows into us, and we now have eternal life.

We can have Eternal Life now.

Eternal life is not just about the future, but we can have it in this world.

Jesus said in John 5:24, "I tell you the truth, listen to me, and believe in the Lord who sent me. He will live forever. He has not been judged, but he has changed from death to life." In other words, immortality is not something to wait for after death. If you believe in Jesus, this is what you have now.

We must believe in the link that bonds us with the life of the Lord in Christ now. If we have Jesus, we have his life now. And his life is everlasting.

Why does eternity exist?

Eternity exists because it takes us a long time to know the infinite glory of God. Two hundred fifty years ago, Jonathan Edwards preached about the experience of seeing eternal life and knowing God forever. He wondered if this was going to get tedious and boring.

The soul is the source of the joy and happiness of seeing God. The understanding can be maximized; it can be done, but it flies to an endless expanse and dives into the bottomless ocean. He may discover more and more of God's beauty and majesty, but he will never run out of wells.

Then he commented on the infinite love of God based on Ephesians 3:18-19. "Enable you to understand all saints, their breadth, length, depth, height; and to understand the love of Christ by knowledge; so that you may be filled with all the abundance of God."

We can never reach the height of (the love of God) by ascending. We can never understand it by descent; or by measurement, we don't know its length and width.

Let your thoughts and wishes expand as you please. There is plenty of space for them to use, where they can grow forever. So, what a blessing to see this man who came to this endless fountain of God! They were lucky to see the face of God, millions of years old, and they would never be bored again. This taste of joy will continue to be refined.

Where are you in the stages of Eternal Life?

Where are you in eternal life? All of you are in at least the second step; listening to the words of life. Here's what I've been saying, and I believe that God has taken many to the third stage. He has attracted you by helping you see the identity of Christ. Oh, you will cross the threshold of life, believe this morning, enter into the eternal life you currently have and have a good relationship with knowing the only true God and Jesus Christ that has been sent.

What if you believe this morning? If you say at last, "Lord Jesus, I will see you in your words and will no longer resist you. I believe in you with my soul and body. I believe in the promise of John 3:16, that is, believing in Christ, He will not perish but will live forever. I received your gift of eternal life."

I really want to know what God has done in your life so we can pray for you. I want to direct you to some helpful guidance to moving forward with Christ.

CHAPTER 09

Understand the Purpose

THE MEANING AND purpose of life are not so easy to understand. Answering some questions involves answering other questions first.

What does it mean to have meaning and purpose? How do you decide what is most important to you? How can you be sure? Can you trust the advice of the people around you to determine your purpose? There are lots of questions and no simple answers.

Okay, let me correct myself. There is a simple answer. Trust in God.

What does the Bible say about the purpose of our lives?

"Everybody who is called by the name (My name), and whom I have formed for My glory, Whom I have created, even whom I have completed" (Isaiah 43:7).

According to the Bible, our purpose here is to glorify God. In other words, we determine to praise God, worship God, proclaim his greatness, and fulfill his will. This is why he is being honored. So, here we see God has given us a reason to exist and given us meaning to exist. He created us according to his wishes, and our life will be lived for him so that we can accomplish all he has done for us. When we trust the One who created us and does all the work under the direction of his will (Ephesians 1:11), then we can live a purposeful life.

The expression of the specific purpose depends on the individual.

Is there any purpose in trials?

What if our life is difficult and things go wrong? Are our failures and hardships also for the glory of God? Yes, I believe that they are. When things go well, we often thank God and praise his name, but when we encounter difficulties, we often give up and complain. Sometimes, our appreciation and trust in God depend on how the situation affects us. In the end, this is immature self-centeredness. Although there may be problems in our lives, our ultimate goal here is to glorify God, even if we experience difficulties. For this, we praise and trust him in difficult times.

In every attempt to glorify God, we can determine God's special meaning for our lives in all aspects. In Christianity, we can pursue God freely in all aspects of life. For example, we are free to honor God by becoming a doctor, lawyer, mechanic, housewife, father, mother, minister, accountant, and so on. If glorifying God is the ultimate goal of life, then we can do this when doing our best in the different calls of life. Therefore, as the Bible says, "... No matter what you do, you must make every effort to honor God" (1 Corinthians 10:31).

Finding the purpose of life

Some people do not believe in God. These are the people who deny that God created us. For them, they want to decide their own purposes.

They decide for themselves what makes sense to them. They want independence. They want to promote the good and bad in their minds and decide their purpose according to their wishes.

But the problem is that this becomes selfish. When we do what we think is right, we often make mistakes; especially when denying God. When a child says, "I want, I want, I want," he shows his immaturity and self-centeredness.

Adults focus on other aspects of life. One in which a lot of sacrifices are made is for the sake of marriage and family. As we mature, we realize the value of considering the interests of others. "Not only pay attention to your own personal interests but also those of others" (Philippians 2:4). In the process, we learn that the best goals are not determined by selfish desires, but more importantly, by love and the ability to think of others. This inherits the will of receiving God. If we are selfish and want to decide our goals, is that love? After all, if love is centered on others, should we not love God?

Live with him as the center, humble himself with his wisdom. Do you believe his desire for us? Think about it. His understanding of us is endless, and by believing in him, we can discover the ultimate purpose of our lives.

Don't just show moralism

Morality does good deeds. Atheists can do this but our goal, as Christians, is not our own glory. Our lives mean glorifying God (Isa. 43:7). Unbelievers do not know God. Therefore, they can only make their own decisions about their meaning and purpose. In other words, they have no objective moral standards other than themselves, so they cannot know their ultimate purpose. Then, at best, they can only adopt a kind of morality, kindness associated with likes and situations, and conditional love. In this way, they do not know what true goodness is. Without knowing what is really good, how can they have good goals in life?

Ways that you are not following the purpose of God

Before investigating this, we need to make at least one warning. In one sense, you have been living in God's will. God is God; he does everything according to his purpose, including your life. Nothing will happen without God's command.

Psalm 57:2 says, "I cry to the Supreme God, the God who executes his will." This is the key to understanding God's will for your life. God has numbered your days, and he will fulfill all his purposes for you.

However, our choices and actions are crucial. In some ways, this is a mystery we cannot fully understand, but this does not mean that we can't understand some parts of it. We can choose to do something that will bring us greater happiness and a greater sense of purpose. This is the reference we are going to discuss in this chapter.

I want to help you determine the choices you can make to bring more excitement and God-given goals to life.

But first, here are six signs that you don't have clear purposes in your life.

1. *You are knowingly living in sin*

Let's start with the obvious. If you clearly disobey the Bible, then you are not living in God's will. You will undoubtedly experience a sense of insignificance in your life. This is straightforward so we don't need to spend too much time here.

2. *Your dearth joy and excitement*

If you wake up with apathy, fear, or boredom every day, then you might not have done what you set out to do. God created you uniquely and planned many wondrous things for you. One of the fruits of the Holy Spirit is joy (Galatians 5:22). Of course, you will encounter difficult things that require patience and perseverance, but in general, you should be full of joy and excitement about your life, work, and relationships.

The hunt for joy in God is not optional. It is not an "additional feature" that a person may grow into after he comes to faith.

3. You don't feel much satisfaction in life

If your life is superficial, you may be departing from God's goal. Achievement comes from doing meaningful, eloquent, and purposeful things. Pursue a job that can use your skills and passion. Relationships that include give and take come from hobbies that are inspirational rather than sensational. Yes, you have to do something boring and unachievable at times, but if you've been gray all your life, you may need to make changes.

You just work for the sake of working

You know the sense of meaningless work. You go to the office, get to work on time, then go home and faint in front of the TV. You work and rest on the weekend. All the real happiness you experience comes from things outside of job. They come from hobbies, friends, or side jobs.

Ecclesiastes 8:15 says, "I want to praise joy because human beings are no happier in the sun than eating, drinking and having fun because, in the life God has given him, his hard work will be together to go with this."

You feel stuck

If you really want change but are completely trapped in your life, it certainly shows that you are not acting according to God's will. The constant desire to be somewhere else but not knowing how to get there is a cry for help to be freed from your circumstance. This freedom can be found if you look to Christ. "If therefore the Son makes you free, you will be free indeed" John 8:36.

You don't have direction

If you do not know God's will for your life, you will continue to feel a sense of purposelessness. You feel like you are hovering between things with no progress. Nothing stimulates your interest, and you have not achieved any specific goals, like the Israelites, who wandered for 40 years after leaving Egypt. They did not progress toward their destination (promised land) until they left their own path and leaned on God's.

Ways to regain purpose in life

1. Go to Lord in prayer

Again, let's start with the obvious. If you feel insignificant, seek wisdom and direction. James 1:5 says, "If any of you lack wisdom, let him ask of God, who shall generously give to all, and it shall be given to the person as well."

It's excellent news that God wants to give you purpose. He wants to provide you with divine wisdom. God doesn't persecute you to cause you pain, he wants you to live a happy, ambitious, and purposeful life. Ask God for clarity of purpose and expect him to give it to you.

2. Dig into his word

The main way God speaks to us is through the Bible. This means that when looking for God's will, the first thing you should do is start studying the Bible. Now, you will not find verses telling you to become a dance instructor or artist, but you will begin to understand the heart of God.

Psalm 119:105 says, "Your word is the lamp at my feet, the light on my way." The Word of God brought the light to what seemed originally dark. In the Bible, you learn how to live wisely in the word of God. This is the first step towards finding a purpose.

3. Determine the gifts and strengths; God has blessed you with

God gives you exceptional gifts and strengths. You may be a math expert or a wise adviser or may have ideas for electronics or business. You may be good at organizing people and finishing work. God's will for you can include things you are already good at.

This is where education is particularly valuable. Going to college or returning to college allows you to discover your gifts and then decide how to use them. It can also connect you with people who want to help you find your goal.

4. Develop your passion

What is your unique passion? In fact, this can be anything from business, art, economics, property, innovation, etc. If money wasn't a problem, what do you want to do?

Deciding on your passion can usually help you find out what God is calling you to do. It is often said that God works at the intersection of our talents and passions. Where does your gift meet your hobby? That may be God's will for you.

5. Bring people into your life

Proverbs 11:14 says, "Where there is no guidance, there are people who are depressed, but where there are many counselors, there is security." One of the main ways in which God helps you find your goal is through others.

A warning here, your adviser should be someone you trust. Whether it's a teacher, parents, or friends, you need someone to support and strive for the best for you. You want a wise counselor to help you find God's will for you.

6. Take an isolation retreat

Sometimes, getting rid of everything and taking some time to think, pray, and write can be very helpful. You don't have to spend a week to make it effective. Even if it's just a day away from the busyness of everyday life, it will bring huge gains.

During these retreats, stay calm. Think deeply. Ask God for direction and listen to his voice. This does not need to be complicated, nor does it require any complex rituals. Hebrews 11:6 reminds us that God always rewards those who seek Him. He does not hide in the dark, trying to hide his will from you. He wants to guide you (Psalm 32:8).

7.   *In the end, have faith in God*

Trying to find your life goals can be stressful. It seems to be such a big, confusing, and frustrating theme. You want to move on, but not sure how. You want to find your goal but feel like you're wandering.

But you can believe God is leading you to where he wants you to go. As Psalm 23:2-3 says, "He led me by the still water. He restored me to the soul. For his name led me to the righteous path." You may be confused, but God is not.

We as Christians

The right way is to give glory to God because no adult is worthy of trust, worship, and admiration. So, as Christians, we want to live and bring glory to God. We do this is by praying and studying his holy word so that we can better understand what he has for us.

CHAPTER 10:

Don't Compromise Integrity for Money or Fame

LIFE WILL ALWAYS bring us an unexpected blow. When we are troubled by such circumstances many of us, let fear decide how we act. This fear destroys our standards. No matter how difficult our situation is, we must always act honestly, not out of fear.

Our honesty and integrity will speak for us. The author of Psalm 26:1 expects the Lord to defend him on the premise of his "travel". Equally, our integrity will bring us protection. In attacking Job at Satan's request, God told him, "Job maintains his integrity."

Our integrity is our way of life, visible and invisible. Whether in church, at home, at work, or in entertainment, we will be known for upholding the moral standards of life. An upright person is a person characterized by moral excellence throughout his life, no matter what happens around him. It seems that their ethical standards are the foundation of their lives.

Therefore, no matter how popular or unpopular we become, we must choose as the psalmists, to walk with integrity. We know that acting with integrity often leads to hard decisions, which make us unwelcome in many places.

I have realized the praise of others is limited and short-lived, but God's reward is endless and eternal. This chapter intends to help you keep your integrity. Keep checking yourself. Let God's Word be the basis for you to judge your standard of living and make immediate adjustments (Titus 2:7). God is not looking for an incredible person to use for his purposes; he's looking for a credible one.

Strong character is a non-negotiable requirement to achieve goals and dreams, the ram that allows us to break through barriers and grow to a better life. Every challenge we face in our journey towards a better life is likely to disappoint us or make us stronger. There is no middle ground. When we face problems and difficulties, it is the strength of our character that allows us to not only face the storm but also turn it into an advantage.

Do your best to be the same person in front of the gathering as you are behind the scenes

When pressure is applied, something always comes out. Under crisis or stress we have lose attention on maintaining our appearance. At those times, our actions reveal who we are — good and bad.

Are you the same person outside work? Do you live differently in different peer groups? Does your environment dictate your speech – or is it consistent? The people who value integrity are the same in all groups. Popularity doesn't matter. Regardless of situation it is important to be able to gain credibility in interactions. You can only achieve this if you have fullness, which is only possible by being the same person in every environment.

Your eccentricity and integrity should support your success, not destroy it. Even if no one is present, good character adheres to right principles. Loyalty to God in your private life is more important than public understanding. Unless you show integrity in small things, he cannot bless you in big things.

Be very cautious not to follow the crowd

You see, true character is what we are talking about – your true identity, not playing a role. You can fake almost everything in life, but you can't put on a facade on your character. You either have good character, or you don't. Character means doing the right thing, no matter what others think. This usually requires standing up for what is right and being brave.

Romans 12:2, "**Do not conform** to the decoration of this world, but be renovated by the renewing of your mind. Then you will be able to check and approve what God's will is—his good, pleasing and perfect will."

Many people talk about having integrity and values, but it is just a cloud of smoke behind their words. There is no substance. When people have more to say about themselves than others, please be careful. This often shows they are actually playing their role.

Be a person who does what he says and leads a life that deserves respect—more than words. Don't become an actor, but a self-evident person, not the other way around. This is where real people are found.

Value the progression of character building

Romans 5:3-5 says, "Not only that, we know that suffering will produce patience, and patience will produce character, and character will produce hope, and hope will not make us feel ashamed, because of our that we have poured out in the love of God, we rejoice for this and enter into our hearts through the Holy Spirit given to us."

This verse is about a character built through patience. If you are an athlete, you will know that there is no shortcut to winning or competing. Character is the same, you can't turn around and grab it. You don't just decide to own it, nor you can tell other people to do it. It is built through endurance.

Don't check your character at the door. Make sure you are always a gentleman or a nobleman, and the rest will follow.

I often say you can reach the peak without integrity. In fact, you may get there faster – however, without strength of character, you will not be able to maintain your height. When you refuse a shortcut, it can take longer to reach your destination, but many valuable resources are waiting. I have learned when I had to wait; my belief, my spiritual foundation, and maturity were the greatest.

God has personality as well as attributes. God's attributes often mentioned are compassion, holiness, righteousness, and mercy, to name but a few. But the Bible also talks about God's character — it has never changed; yesterday, today, and forever. He is trustworthy, true, and loyal. His character is something one can depend on it. His words are eternal. As a God of integrity, he longs for the integrity of his followers.

Integrity is a God-like life of reliability and sincerity, with no deception or tricks. Integrity's dominant quality is completeness. In fact, the word integrity is extracted from the same root word as integer, meaning whole. In simple terms, no difference exists between one's public life and one's private life. People who value integrity have nothing to hide and have nothing to fear.

Acting honesty creates a reputation. Integrity reflects the sum of our existence and actions. Integrity is not what we have, but what we are. It inevitably manifests in what we do and what we say. People are watching us. Will our actions conform to our beliefs? Will our character match our confession?

Authenticity

The adage is correct, our walk has to fit into our conversation. Our way of life must match our family, churches, and friends. Everybody must know who we say we are. There should be no fraud or deception in our lives. When everything is lost, our name, reputation, and character are going to live on. For our church, our family, and our lives, we need a fulfilling life. In fact, integrity is just as important as mental health, family priorities, and personal development. In the long run, integrity is fundamental.

For people to live an upright life, they must act in a real way. Paul instructed the Philippians, "Before Christ comes, be sincere and innocent" (Philippians 1:10). Sincerity is a Latin word meaning "no-wax". It originated in the market of ancient Rome. If someone wanted a truly high-quality sculpture carved by someone proud of their craftsmanship, they would venture to the handicraft market in Rome Quad to look for signs marked "sine cera" or " no wax". Wax and marble were mixed to patch imperfections. You can find real things at the "Sine Ceramics" booth. No bugs, no covers, no behind-the-scenes transactions.

Honest men and women are hard people to find. Such people have no hidden flaws nor hidden agenda. These are the people who portray their real selves.

Honesty

One way authenticity discloses itself is by always speaking the truth. Make a note of a couple of proverbs:

"The LORD detests lying lips, but he delights in people who are trustworthy." (Proverbs 12:22 NIV)

"The integrity of the upright guides them, but the unfaithful are destroyed by their duplicity." (Proverbs 11:3, NIV).

When we speak the truth, we reflect the character of God, because "God ... will not lie" (Titus 1:2).

"That ye may walk honestly toward them that are without, and *that* ye may have lack of nothing." (I Thessalonians 4:12 KJV).

Honesty has always been difficult to find. The Greek philosopher Diogenes lit a candle during the day and then traveled to find an honest person. Blaise Pascal said he didn't expect to meet three honest people in a century. The Behavioral Incentive Institute found that 97 out of 100 people lie and do it about 1,000 times a year.

Honesty is like a boomerang. Our words and who we are, are always walking around. Each time an individual engages in any dishonest activity, the outcome will come back to them. Ask any politician about the closet skeleton. Honest people are different. They are such a rare breed that even if they pay the price, they still deliver on their promises, keep their promises, and tell the truth.

Telling the truth always wins. The author of Proverbs says, "Whoever walks in integrity walks securely, but whoever takes crooked paths will be found out." (Proverbs 10:9, NIV). When the facts are reported, nothing will bother us again.

Conviction

Integrity is not only about authenticity and truth, but it is also about faith. An upright person represents the right thing. Without deep conviction, one cannot stand as an upright person. They know their beliefs and reasons. Beliefs are not imposed on individuals; they are internal beliefs and actions.

"Faith is the main force for action and the motivation for life. A person's life is their faith." Martin Luther King Jr. told his children, "If a person has nothing worth dying for, then he is not fit for life."

Faith must be based on the knowledge of the truth, as stated in the Bible. The knowledge of righteousness needed to shape our beliefs comes from a full understanding of God's Word. Without understanding and practicing biblical principles, we wither like grass in the fire of temptation.

God wants his followers to live a life of integrity, though it is not easy. Living a character like God, being the same in private and in public, and fulfilling our faith — faithful to the teachings of the Bible — is difficult and uncomfortable. In a world that (sometimes) accepts praise for lack of criticism; choosing truth, honesty, and firm belief is always a challenge. However, integrity affects us and affects those around us, especially our children. We can clearly see the impact of our conviction is when we look at the impression we leave on children and their children.

CHAPTER 11:

Evangelize Life

TODAY, EVANGELISM HAS considerable buzz. Jesus commanded us to go and make disciples of all nations, Mathew 28:19, but most of us do not quite know what this actually means. Evangelism proclaims the gospel — good news about Jesus Christ, the power of God to save every believer in Jesus and to turn from sin to follow him.

So in this chapter, we will discuss some of the practical tips to evangelize in our life.

1. Pray for people by name

You already know someone who hasn't heard the good news (gospel). When you pray, call their name before God. God "does more work in our hearts than everything we ask or think of." (Ephesians 3:20). "I urge, then, first of all, that petitions, prayers, intercession and thanksgiving be made for all people," (1 Timothy 2:1). Prayer brings opportunities to share faith with them and believe that God has established a relationship with you in these conversations.

2. Go out into all God's creations

Don't just socialize in the "bubble." Like-minded friends are essential in nurturing our beliefs, but never forget the responsibility to invite others to join the family. Jesus tells us of his great mission, "Therefore, make disciple of all nations." (Matthew 28:19). While it is undoubtedly more comfortable to spend time with other Christians, we are asked to step out of our immediate circle and reach out to those who will never receive an invitation unless we reach out to them. Jesus is incarnate and lives among us. We follow his example, when we meet other classmates, coworkers, or neighbours; whether in the classroom, sports team, club, lunch room, or park.

3. Be Bold

It can be scary to introduce yourself to someone you don't know. Ask the Holy Spirit to give you what you need. "For the Holy Spirit will teach you in that very hour what you ought to say." (Luke 12:12 NKJV) Have courage! At first glance, it may seem embarrassing, but as we want to say, "Heaven is worth embarrassing!"

4. Extend Personal Invites

How many invitations do you have on Facebook events now? How many times do you actually plan to participate? The event you attend is likely to be something that someone takes time to invite you to. Invite someone to host an event with you! Your personal invitation may attract people who need friends.

5. Share life with everyone & be with them in their activities

Find things that you and your friends can do together, even if this is not something you like doing. Sacrifice your choices to do what you do not like. Evangelism is not just an intellectual endeavor! When you spend time with friends and do what they love, you get the privilege to listen. Your friends will trust your recommendations for movies, books, restaurants, etc. They will see that your life is different — the joy, trust, and confidence in Jesus make you different, and they want to know why.

6. Share your narrative

Your story is powerful! If you haven't yet, considered writing out how you came to know Jesus. How did you decide to pursue it? St. Peter tells us, "Always be ready to respond to all who ask you to give a reason for hope." (1 Peter 3:15) No one can argue with what you have experienced, so be ready to share with others when someone asks.

7. Practice hospitality everywhere you are

You can reassure others with simple, friendly behavior, such as starting the conversation first or introducing new friends to everyone else in the group. Hospitality doesn't always mean you have to bring pizza, but you can invite someone quiet to make the first move.

8. Share the gospel with a definite invitation

Sharing the gospel is the core of evangelism! There are many ways to share the story of Jesus, but the core of the gospel contains four main points:
1. You have a relationship with God.
2. Sin (when we choose not to love) creates a gap between you and God.
3. God became a man in Jesus and died for your sins to repair your relationship with God.
4. When one accepts God's invitation, he has an opportunity to establish a relationship with God!

When you share these views with someone in conversation, you can encourage your friends with ask questions like, "Are you ready to invite Jesus to be the center of your life?" If they are not ready, let them know that you are still their friend, and continue to pray for them. If they agree, please celebrate and pray with them!

9. Seek out Christ together

Your friend's commitment to Jesus as the center of life is not a one-time deal. Now you can go to the goal together to heaven.

Continue to invite them to spend time with you and get to know Jesus more deeply. This can mean going on a retreat or business trip, attending a focus-seeking meeting, and attending anything you love together — of course, continuing to spend time doing what you like.

10. Show others to do the same

Friends you teach, must preach the gospel too, and do it together! St. Paul wrote, "What you hear from me ... I believe in faithful people who can teach others too" (1 Timothy 2:2). Jesus chose apostles who could teach others. You can fulfill the mission of evangelism by building deep friendships, inviting people to follow Jesus, and teaching others to do the same!

CHAPTER 12:

Be Generous to Others

WE NEED TO understand, as Proverbs 11-25 says, a generous person will prosper, whoever refreshes others will be refreshed.

We all have reasons for not giving or helping others. Common barriers to generosity are pride, greed, debt, stinginess, and busyness.

Pride says we worked hard for everything we have, so these are ours and ours. We blame the poor for their situation thinking they are lazy or using us when they need help.

Greed shows as always wanting more no matter whether we need it or not, and it never just seems enough. For lack of satisfaction, we prefer to take rather than to give.

Debt makes you a slave to the lender. How do you give freely? Financial debt has a way of stifling generosity because our resources are used for monthly payments and high interest rates!

Stinginess comes from a fear of lack. There is an ingrained bias to calculate the potential return for each amount we give. The motivation is to gain something. If we are prepared to pay, we want to make sure no one can get more than they deserve. We start by saying, "what's in it for me?"

Being busy distracts us and we don't have time to help and think about what we can do for others. We often engage in self-centered activities, hobbies, and attempts to numb ourselves, and we rarely worry about our neighbors needing help. We spend too much time being busy because we don't have time to help and think about what we can do for others.

Why do we need to give?

For all of the above reasons, you may remember that sharing is the first lesson your parents taught you as a child. Our parents understand the blessings of those who give to others. This is often difficult to understand when we are young, but as we mature in the Christian life sharing is the result of faith and relationship with God.

What you need to understand to be generous

When you walk with the Lord, generosity should come naturally. You should be able to understand yourself and understand what God has done for you. To become generous, you need to understand something of God's Word.

1. You are God's child

When you become a Christian, you are a child of God, and God is the ultimate giver. Generosity begins. God is love, and love is the motivation that gave us his most precious son, Jesus Christ, to die for us, that we may not perish but have eternal life (John 3:16).

As a child of God, you have his nature now. Now, generosity already exists in your DNA. As disciples and followers of Christ, we will follow the example of Jesus giving us life. God told us to imitate him. "Be holy, as I am holy" (1 Peter 1:16).

We often hear the comment, "As a father, as a son." This is usually the case. People think that the child's behavior shows what kind of parents they have. If we claim to be Christians, then we must walk godly – in God's example.

We are God's children, so we should naturally reflect his character in the way we live. When we surrender to the inner Holy Spirit and focus more on who we are than on what we have, our generosity becomes apparent.

2. Giving comes from the inside

Gifts are things that concern hearts, not wallets. This is how we trust God more than money. In the book of second Corinthians, we learn the story of the Macedonian church. Although the Macedonian church was impoverished, they begged Paul to allow them help the suffering Christians in Jerusalem. This makes no sense whatever.

Unsurprisingly, Macedonians did not believe that a lack of money is an excuse for not participating in rescue work. When they learned that the believers in Jerusalem needed help, they volunteered to help. To them, this was a natural reaction. They acted per God's way of doing things.

The Bible proclaims, "They did not do what we expected, but by God's will they gave themselves to the Lord and then to us" (1 Corinthians 8:5). That is a secret. Their heart surrendered to God, and the wallet followed.

3. You have an unlimited source

Your giving is based on your view of God. It is infinite. The earth is Lord, everything on earth (Psalm 24:1). The Bible says heaven is his throne, and earth is his footstool (Isaiah 66:1).

If you know the true identity and strength of God, you live without a doubt. However, if you think the Lord will run out of resources, you will always be stingy.

People do not share because they do not believe God will provide everything they need. Our God is not a "flawed God" but a "more than enough" God. When we bless others, God will take care of our needs. As 2 Corinthians 9:8 says, "And Lord can bless you abundantly, so that in all things at all times, having all that you require, you will abound in every good work."

4. Giving is a chance to change lives

The Bible explains to us that we are blessed not just so that we can feel satisfied and happy and not just so we can be pleased and comfortable, but so that we will bless others. Our blessings should pour into others.

1 John 3:17 proclaims, "If anybody has material possessions and sees his brother in need but has no feelings on him, how can the love of Lord be in him?"

If you are a Christian, then God will give you grace and express sympathy through sacrifice. Love and goodness are the gifts of the Holy Spirit. Ask the Lord what he wants you to do. This prayer opened the eyes of the king. You can't do everything, but you can do something! This attitude makes you discover that your generosity is not based on limited ability but the supernatural power of God.

The example of God's selfless gift to Jesus opens us with the opportunity to become the Son of God. He saw the depths of sin and cleared it through his son Jesus. Our future depends on sowing today. Paul said, "Do not be deceived; God cannot be mocked. A person harvests the sown food" (Galatians 6:10). Bless others and you are happy. It benefits both the one who gives and the one who receives.

Generosity has nothing to do with money. This is about helping people in need. Whenever money is involved (for example, who gave how much), generosity loses its purity and no longer acts as God intended. God is happy for happy giving. God invites us to be a part of the great work he has done to change people's lives. He invites us to work with Him. Think about how your generous ways can change the lives of others, work hard for the glory of Christ, and then do it again!

May our hearts excess with humble, creative generosity because God in Christ has first been generous to us.

CHAPTER 13:

Helping as Much as You Can

SINCE THE BIRTH of Christianity serving others has been a Christian virtue. Jesus himself was a suffering servant. He emphasized this truth when washing the feet of the disciples in the upper room. If our master Jesus gave his life to others, how can we expect us to do less? More importantly, he told us that the world would know that we are his disciples because of our love for one another. The truth is that serving others can be more than just doing it. Let's take a look.

To help others is the essence of being a Christian. Christianity is not only a religion but also a way of life. This shows that people can know that we are Christians through our way of life. Unfortunately, this is often not the case.

Miracle at Cana

Every aspect of Jesus' earthly life helped others. When you look closely, even his first miracle in Cana lies in helping those in need. You might ask how families running out of wine at a wedding can be considered as role models of the unfortunate!

However, like many other things, this must be considered in

the social context of the age. Running out of wine means the host has nothing to give, which will bring shame to the family's name. This marriage would always be noted with shame. The host family is ashamed, and the newly married couple will be humiliated in society for the rest of their life. There is no doubt that this family in Cana would eventually become some of those unfortunate people.

Calvary

Calvary was the destiny of Jesus as a child in Bethlehem. The evil Judas played his role, and when Christ himself asked to take this cup from him in the Garden of Gethsemane, he immediately expressed great emotion.

In giving his life for our salvation, he played the most significant role and expressed his love for us. Although it is evident that Christians are being persecuted for faith in many parts of the world today, it is unlikely any of us will be required to be sacrificed because of our faith.

So, what precisely are we being requested to do, and how can we display it on an ongoing basis each day?

Love your neighbor

Any attempt to act in a Christian way is becoming more and more difficult. The essence of Christianity is community. The basic principle is that we love our neighbors as we love ourselves. However, in these times we live in, people pay more attention to personal worship and self-control. The saying is "succeed at all costs".

It is said that one of the reasons communism does not work is that people are reluctant to share with others. I think the implication is distrust — we're always afraid of each other. As Christians, we are required to think and act in exactly the opposite way. Indeed, this is all-inclusive.

Challenges

Christianity challenges us to change from a comfortable lifestyle to putting the needs of others before ourselves. Jesus made it clear that our treatment of the poor is a standard we set for our treatment.

In the words of Mother Teresa, "Among the poor, we see Jesus in disguise." Drugs, alcohol, and prostitution oppress the poor and they often face ruthless bureaucracy, racial discrimination, and selfishness. Economic reasons and the desire to maintain the upper-class elements hinder real change.

You may be wondering how much contact with the poor we really have in our daily lives. There are many "bad" ways; the bullied child in school, people who have no friends at work, the widow next door who is scared and alone. I think we can all give an example of unfortunate people we know.

God not only demands that we raise awareness, but that we also seek to reduce the burden on people. For example, we may think that giving beggars money will not really benefit in the long run; but we may consider volunteering with groups that help the homeless.

We care about those unfortunate people because God wants us to, and he shows us how to live his son's gift of love. We need to care for others in the way of Jesus and save those in need and suffering from wherever we meet them.

Benefits of helping others

You may have heard the word "love your neighbor" many times, and it has lost its meaning and influence. Also, we live in such an individualistic society that it is easy to fall into our dilemmas most of the time, without even paying attention to our neighbors. The Bible is clear, our motivation should always be love for Christ, and serving and helping others is also good for personal growth in Christ. Consider the following five ways:

1) *Improves the focus of your mind*

Serving others will force you to turn your attention away from yourself. In the final analysis, we're all in the same boat and usually just focus on ourselves. This is why helping others has such a huge spiritual benefit. The more you look away from yourself, the more you see other people, the more you see God around you.

2) Practice what you are reading

The Bible is full of spiritual insights, principles of life, and invaluable wisdom. It is powerful, unprecedented, and can change lives. You can read the same passage over and over again in your life, and you can find valuable insights you have never seen before.

3) Join God in his work

When you serve others, you are doing the work with the Lord. He has been working around you. When you ask God, "What can I do?" He says, "Come with me. I'm already doing it." Sometimes you just need to open your eyes and remove the blindness from your life; you will find countless opportunities. Neighbors are blessings. You do not have to be in a top position. You can join in the Lord's work today just by helping the neighbor.

Serve and help others, dear Christian, as a response to his love, and keep in mind always that you are serving our God Jesus.

4) God will change the heart

This is beyond doubt. The moment you step out and help others God will change your heart. You may feel you will be a blessing to others, and you will. But often you will feel that you could be someone more wonderful. God has been working around you, but he is also extremely interested in your inner things.

5) Have everlasting significance

When you serve God from a heart that loves God and imitates his heart, your actions will resonate in eternity. This is not an exaggeration, this is biblical.

Whatever you do, you must do things for God, not for humanity, because you know that you will receive your inheritance back from

God. You serve the Lord Christ. Colossians 3:23-24 (see also Matthew 6:1-6)

Dear Christians, serve others, respond to his love, remember that you have been serving our Lord Jesus. And, don't seek recognition, or it will be your only reward. Pay attention to the kingdom. Stay focused on God.

As believers of Jesus Christ, we don't have to look far to understand the ultimate example of what it means to serve and help others. Christ's entire life, though brief on earth, illustrated the deeds of serving others; when he healed the sick, when he got on his knees and washed the believer's feet, and when he laid down his whole life to give all a hope and a future.

As much of Jesus's life and ministry was devoted to serving and helping others, it only makes sense that these attributes should also be a significant part of our lives.

1. Where you use your money affects your cheerfulness

The University of British Columbia and Harvard Business School conducted a study on how a person's spending affects their mood. A total of 640 Americans were interviewed and questioned to report their income, their monthly spending comprising all bills and money spent on themselves, their over-all happiness, and gifts given to others or charities. The results were surprising.

Irrespective of an individual's income, people who spent more money on others or gave to charities described higher levels of contentment and pleasure than those who didn't.

Verse to reflect on: Acts 20:35 In all that I have displayed you that by working hard in this manner you should help the weak and recollect the words of the God Jesus, that he himself stated, 'It is more sacred to give than to receive.'"

2. Helping others benefits your health

As per the study conducted by Doug Oman of the University of California, Berkley, older people who volunteer for two or more organizations were 45% less likely to die over a five-year span than those who didn't volunteer.

Another research study observed that individuals who provided communal support to others had lower blood pressure than those who didn't. It suggests that serving others may have a direct physiological advantage as well.

Verse to reflect on Romans 12:13 "Share with Lord's people who are in need. Practice friendliness."

When we show compassion, love, and kindness towards others, what we are doing two things: 1) Practicing the same compassion, love, and kindness that God displayed toward us, 2) Representing one of the main messages of the Gospel, which is to help and serve others.

3. Serving others brings us closer together

When we help others, it not only enables others to feel closer to us but also helps us feel closer to them as well. Being generous and kind leads you to perceive others more charitably and positively.

Verse to reflect on: Acts 4:32 "All the followers were one in mind and heart. No one demanded that any of his possessions was his own, but they shared all they had."

As Lord is the giver of all gifts (Psalm 24:1), we need to understand that our properties are really not our own and we are just caretakers (Matthew 25:21) of his provisions.

We, as Christians, must be of a parallel heart and mind; that is absorbed in loving and helping the way Jesus Christ did. It must be no surprise that when we serve others, it helps in bonding us, aids us to grow closer together in companionship, and promotes more compassion and love towards each other.

4. Assisting others promotes more thankfulness in our lives

When we give the gift of serving others or are on the receiving end of that gift, we experience moods of thankfulness most of the time.

As per the study, college students who counted their blessings experienced more thankfulness in their lives, which caused them to be more positive, exercise more, and feel better about their lives overall.

Verse to reflect on 2 Corinthians 2:14 "So, as we are receiving a kingdom that cannot be shaken, let us be grateful, and so worship God acceptably with respect and awe."

Do you remember the last time you saw someone giving food to a homeless person or someone opening the door for a stranger? What feelings did it provoke?

Daily we have a choice that moves us more towards love, or more towards stress. When we choose compassion in the form of serving others, our hearts are usually filled with feelings of thankfulness. This study only demonstrates how big of a difference serving others can make in our own lives.

5. Giving spreads to others

One more Harvard study observed that when individuals give to others, it inspires others to do the same, which increases the effect of giving.

Verse to reflect on: Titus 2:7 "In everything set an example by doing what is moral."

So, we must help and serve others, just the way Jesus showed us.

Still growing in Christ

No matter where you walk in the Lord, you are always growing until his blessed days have brought us all back. During this time, stay in touch with other Christians, read the Bible and pray, and then go out to serve others. Come and be inspired! No matter where you are, your life really begins.

CHAPTER 14:

Stewardship, A
Way of Life

EVERYONE CAN AGREE that terrible managers are not a good for an organization. If management is not right, everyone will suffer, and things will become chaotic. Also, people will get confused, and information will be missed, then productivity starts declining. Overall, poor management can lead to massive chaos. Good managers give priority to the people or tasks they are given. They model services and are selfless. They set standards of excellence for others.

In fact, we are all managers. Yes, even young people who may feel they have few responsibilities in this stage of life. God has entrusted us with many things, and he wants us to be good stewards. The literal translation of the word "steward" is manager. We are called to be responsible managers, whether it's money, time, interpersonal relationships, talents, or even God's green earth.

How are you dealing with the things God has placed in your care?

As you consider this imperative for your life and all that God has entrusted to you, keep these things in mind when organizing your God-given responsibilities:

1. *God is in charge*

Psalm 24:1 reminds us, "The earth is God's land, all that is in it, the world and all the people who live in it (NIV)." In James we learn, "All acts of generosity, all-perfect gifts are all from above" (HCSB, 1:17). As human beings who often take on the goals of fame, property, and power, we must humble ourselves daily and recognize that God is our creator and sustainer. When we believe in his arrangement, God will give us what we need.

2. *Honesty is the best strategy*

Manipulation and deception are Satan's strategies trying to lure us off the path of becoming good rulers. Don't let Satan win! 1 Corinthians 4:2 (ESV) reminds us, "Also, the steward must prove their reliability."

3. *We need each other*

When we all use God's gifts, everyone benefits. We learned in 1 Corinthians 12:6-7 (MSG), "Everyone has something to do to show who God is; everyone is involved and everyone benefits. The Holy Spirit takes all sorts of things and shares them with all kinds of people! The variety is great." When we strive to be good managers, we have to work together and appreciate the different abilities, talents, and skills that everyone has.

If you strive for it, you can become a good manager. It's not always easy, not always fun. But in the end, our responsibility towards God still exists. Choose to be a good manager. When you make yourself a top priority for others, you glorify God and set an effective standard for those around you. You will also bring additional standards into the future seasons of life.

What do we mean by "stewardship"?

A Christian steward realizes God is the source of all things and knows that we are responsible for how we use the gifts he has entrusted to us.

Stewardship is based on the Bible. It is as old as the Old Testament and is an integral part of our faith today. According to the 1992 USCCB Pastor's Foster Care Letter, a Christian steward is, "A person gratefully receives the gift of God, cherishes and nurtures them in a responsible way, shares justice and love with others, and takes back to the Lord."

The giftedness

God gives each of us unique gifts in many ways. When we attribute talents to God and dedicate them to him, it is not pride or arrogance to have these gifts, but true humility.

Our unique gifts include our lives and time spent, our beliefs and churches, our relationships, our jobs and occupations, our abilities and interests, our experience and passion, our talents and personalities, our money and property, the environment, and our citizenship — even our obstacles, weaknesses, and mistakes.

Once we realize how generous God is to us, we will be grateful and work to develop all our gifts and realize our full potential. We put them to good use; to serve others, build God's kingdom, and share generously in proportion to what he has previously given.

Gratitude, Generosity, Responsibility, and Accountability

There are just four dimensions of good stewardship-irrespective of the type of stewardship in question; gratitude, generosity, responsibility, and accountability. So, we might ask ourselves some questions:

While I believe that God makes me talented, will I pay for my talents?

Should I be responsible for my time?

Am I generous with my treasures?

Am I responsible for land and water management?

We are each responsible for our own lives and response to the special circumstances God has endowed for us. The Bible says to us the Lord loves cheerful givers. Our generosity should be unconditional, and we are happy to provide gifts. At some point, we are all asked to explain how we use the gifts entrusted to us by God — how we respond to God's generosity in our lives.

We worry that if we give our time, we won't have enough time to do what we want. We fear that if we give our money, we won't have enough money to buy what we want for loved ones and ourselves. We worry that if we give our talent, we won't be able to meet our expectations. We are concerned that if we love unconditionally, we won't get enough rewards. Our consumer-centric society tells us that we will never have "enough" things. We will always have to buy more and to do more.

Christian management is counter cultural. It's called the "antidote to materialism." We Christians believe that God has given each of us "enough". That it is precisely what we need to realize the plan that he has for us.

Similarly, we also know that if we share, we will have "enough" opportunities! No matter how small or limited our gifts, if we generously share them, God will "do" with what we provide, just as Jesus took a few loaves of bread and fish and to make it "enough" to feed everyone!

The right to manage is to distinguish our needs from wants, to demand simplicity, and to prioritize life. We use valuable time and resources for what really matters. Control is our belief, which

is reflected in our daily lives. We must believe God will always provide what we need and believe we can live the life of a disciple, as he
said, and believe that when we fail because of human weakness, he
will still provide comfort. He lifts us and helps us try again.

Time, Talent, and Treasure

No matter what our living conditions or requirements, we
all have the same number of hours each day. Making the most of
this time requires maintaining our priorities. Due to limited time,
whenever we say "yes" to something, we have to say "no" to other
things. We need to make "yes" our highest priority.

A simple and profound way to be a good steward of God's
time is to attend holy communion regularly and establish a good
prayer life. Even those in your congregation who feel unable to con-
tribute in any other way can pray for the church, the world, their
community, and individuals in the community.

Christian discipline shows us that everything comes from
God, including our wealth and the ability to create our wealth. It's
really free to just release some of the things we borrowed. It allows
us to follow the teachings of Jesus more closely.

To be a good steward of God's money and property entrusted
to us, we are required to honestly differentiate our needs from our
wants. God always provides what we need, but he rarely provides
everything we want.

If we do not intend to return the "first fruit" from God after
taking care of our own and many selfish needs, we will leave the
rest to God alone. This is why making an annual giving plan is so
important to our discipline. Sometimes people ask what the tiniest
gift is. But why do we consider the smallest obligation to God, who
gives us everything? We at least need to share it with others out
of our deep gratitude and love for God. Making your gift holy or
sacrificial is enough to change your lifestyle. Don't "pay until you
get hurt," but pay until you feel good!

To order more copies of this book, find books by other
Canadian authors, or make inquiries about publishing
your own book, contact PageMaster at:

PageMaster Publication Services Inc. 11340-120 Street,
Edmonton, AB T5G 0W5
books@pagemaster.ca
780-425-9303

catalogue and e-commerce store **PageMasterPublishing.ca/
Shop**

About the Author

KIDANE ARAYA WAS born in Adi-mekeda, Eritrea in 1972. He grew up on a farm and despite experiencing its benefits he knew that being a businessman was in his future. In the late nineties, Kidane opened a textile firm in Adi-mekeda but later decided he wanted a more wholesome life for his family. He moved to Germany to further his studies and eventually brought his family there as well. In 2013 Kidane and his family became Canadian citizens.

Kidane attributes his progress and the actualization of his dream to settle in Canada to the inspiration and stalwart support of his wife, Tsege Ghebretinsae.

In 2007, Kidane opened All Canada Clean Corp. and it has flourished into a thriving business today. He has also started many businesses in Ethiopia, Uganda, Dubai, China and Europe.

Kidane has learned life-fulfilling lessons by through business. He now wishes to pass on his life-long learnings, about how starting a business is a viable venture and well worth the efforts. But more importantly, he wants to emphasize the keys to achieving success which are applying faith to daily life, staying inspired yourself, and having a supportive family.

www.ingramcontent.com/pod-product-compliance
Lightning Source LLC
LaVergne TN
LVHW021539080426
835509LV00019B/2730